AMERICAN NATURE GUIDES
BUTTERFLIES
OF
NORTH AMERICA

AMERICAN NATURE GUIDES
BUTTERFLIES
OF
NORTH AMERICA

JOHN FELTWELL
Illustrations by
BRIAN HARGREAVES

SMITHMARK

This edition first published in the United States in 1992 by
SMITHMARK Publishers Inc.,
16 East 32nd Street, New York, NY 10016.

Published in England by Dragon's World Ltd, Limpsfield and London.

ISBN 0-8317-6963-7

SMITHMARK books are available for bulk purchase for sales
promotions and premium use. For details write or call the manager
of special sales, SMITHMARK Publishers Inc.,
16 East 32nd Street, New York, NY 10016: (212) 532-6600.

EDITOR Michael Downey
DESIGN James Lawrence
ART DIRECTOR Dave Allen
EDITORIAL DIRECTOR Pippa Rubinstein

Typeset by Dorchester Typesetting, Dorchester, England
Printed in Singapore

Contents

Introduction

Butterflies are everywhere in North America. They have exploited every habitat from the stifling tropics to the chilly wastes of Alaska, Greenland, and Baffin Island, and a wide variety of man-made habitats too. People who watch wildlife soon realize that there is a great diversity of butterflies just waiting to be studied. And further research is badly needed, since there are scores of butterflies whose life-cycles or foodplants are unknown. Thus there is a real need for a nature guide to pack in the knapsack or carry in the hip pocket and to bring out at a moment's notice to identify a butterfly on a flower or basking on a rock. There is always a chance you will discover an interesting piece of butterfly biology. It is best to use a nature guide in the field rather than to kill a butterfly and identify it later at home.

The appeal of a concise nature guide such as this is that, wherever your travels take you throughout the United States of America (USA) or Canada, the common species will be present in this book.

Butterflies are not always easy to identify in the field. With some experience it is possible to place a butterfly in its correct family because of its characteristic wing shape and general color design, or from the way it flies. However, it might be impossible to make a satisfactory identification of a small skipper or hairstreak, simply because the insect does not keep still long enough, or because there is a whole group of related species which have similar colors and patterns. Here a net is useful to capture the butterfly in order to look closely at its markings. After inspection, the butterfly can be liberated.

The other great factor which hinders identification is individual variation. The specimen captured may not be completely typical, individual variation may have made this specimen look like another closely-related species, and it will not therefore look like the figure illustrated in this book, since only typical specimens have been illustrated.

The butterflies described in this book are those which are found within the New World (Nearctic) region, a biogeographic area whose southern boundary runs somewhat wavily through Mexico. Most of the butterflies found in the United States are included, with the exception of a hundred or so which straddle the United States/Mexican boundary, or which are strays into

the United States from Mexico or the Antillean Islands. A few
Hawaiian species are also included since this is one of the 50
states, and it lies in the northern hemisphere at the interface
between two geographic regions, one of them the New World.

There are at least 750 species of butterfly in the New World,
and that is without considering other species resident in Mexico
but which do not penetrate the United States. Excluding the
strays which venture north from Mexico, and those whose
distribution straddles the boundary, the number of butterflies
described in this book is a little over 400 species. This makes a
comprehensive assemblage of the commoner butterflies likely
to be found. Such is the specialized distribution of some
butterflies, and the vagaries of their occurrence, that no one
person is ever likely to see all the butterflies listed, flying free in
their own habitats – a sobering thought. And a number of
northern butterflies fly only in alternate years.

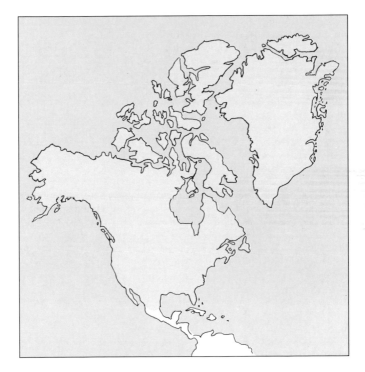

The New World (Nearctic), including part of Mexico. The
area covered in this volume is shaded gray.

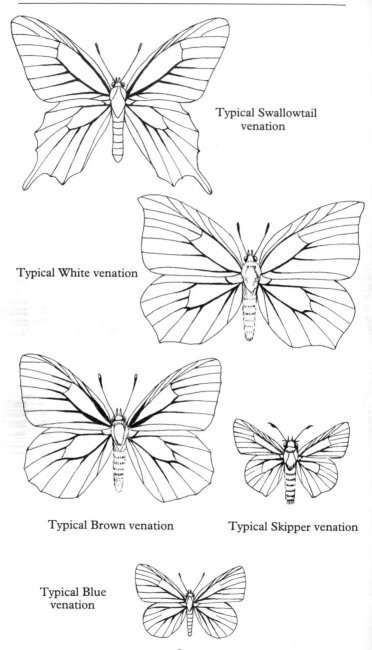

Typical Swallowtail venation

Typical White venation

Typical Brown venation

Typical Skipper venation

Typical Blue venation

The illustrations in this book are more comprehensive than in any previous publication. They include the uppersides markings of each sex of each species, the male's upper wings illustrated on the left of each composition, the female's on the right. About a third of the species are also accompanied with an illustration of the undersides. The sex which has the most useful identification features was usually chosen for illustration of the undersides.

The order of the butterfly families strictly follows the latest scientific knowledge. However, there is one exception; the swallowtails begin the book and are placed there for aesthetic reasons, since they are so colorful.

Each butterfly is given a common (or trivial) name in English and a scientific Latin one. Sometimes an alternative common name is given which may well be of equal standing. If there are further common names, which is often the case, these are not given. A good working knowledge of Latin allows one to get more out of the names since many are highly descriptive of the butterfly colors, patterns, or behavior, or of the habitat.

For each species details of four items are given: identification features, habitat, flight period, and distribution. Notes on identification relate to key shapes, markings, sexual differences, and the degree to which individual and seasonal variations can cause problems in identification. If several subspecies of a species exist, this is simply noted at the end of the 'identification' sentence with 'variable as subspecies'; this is to draw attention to the potential difficulty in identifying specimens which may be significantly different from the subspecies illustrated. Some subspecies look wildly different from the norm, there are a number with more than ten subspecies, and the Western Checkerspot even has 17 subspecies. If distinct races or seasonal forms exist which might hinder identification, these are often mentioned as well.

Habitat types are mentioned since these can be helpful clues to identification, if only because the foodplant may be an integral part of that habitat.

The flight period, or period when the butterfly may be expected to be on the wing, is a useful aid in identification and also in planning forays into the countryside to study butterflies. Both the period when the insect is likely to be seen and the number of generations that the butterfly has each year are given under this section. If there is no clear break between each of the generations such that they overlap, then the term 'continuous' is used and the earliest and latest period given. Generally speaking, fewer generations are found toward the north, and more toward the south. Typical examples are species which have two generations in the south and only one in the north, or

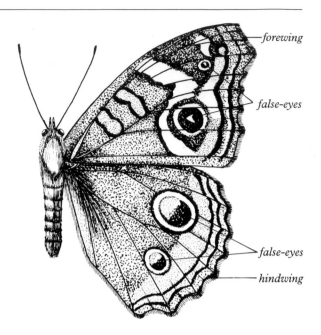

The familiar Buckeye showing its lively false-eyes
(or eye-spots) on both the forewing and hindwing

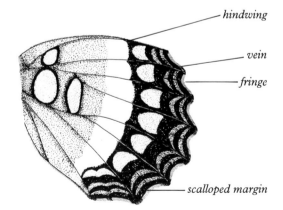

Scalloped hindwing of a White Admiral showing indented
margin

Underside hindwing of a Zebra Swallowtail showing an extra long 'tail', elongated hindwing shape, and scalloped margin

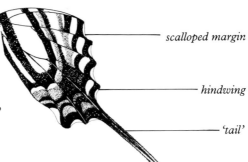

— scalloped margin

— hindwing

— 'tail'

Underside hindwing of a Dotted Blue showing fringe, margin, and spots

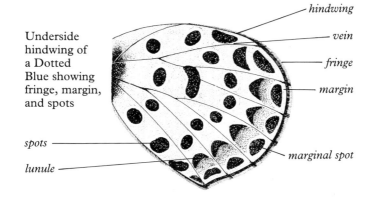

— hindwing

— vein

— fringe

— margin

spots —

lunule —

— marginal spot

hindwing base —

Hindwing underside of the Blue and Gray Hairstreak showing two unequal length 'tails' and indented inside edge of wing

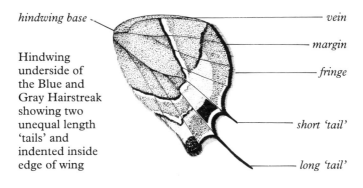

— vein

— margin

— fringe

— short 'tail'

— long 'tail'

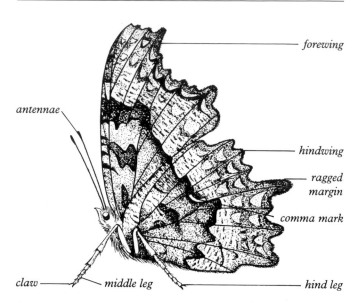

forewing

antennae

hindwing

ragged margin

comma mark

claw — middle leg — hind leg

Side view of undersides of the Green Comma showing two functional legs, ragged nature of wing margins, and camouflage design

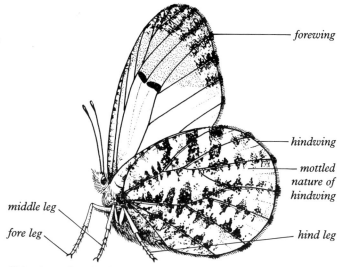

forewing

hindwing

mottled nature of hindwing

middle leg

fore leg

hind leg

Side view of underside of the Western Orange Tip showing three functional legs and mottled camouflage pattern of hindwing

three in the south and two in the north. In a similar manner populations at high altitudes will have a later flight period than those at lower altitudes, and fewer generations.

The great diversity of North American topography means that a general statement such as 'one generation, May to August' (abbreviated to 'one, May–August') could be different at sea level from that at a high altitude. The warmer and lower the site, the earlier the emergence; the higher and colder, the later. So butterfly haunts vary in terms of the ecological constraints which they impose on insects, and when we might find them. There may also be 'early' and 'late' sites in the same neighborhood, even on different sides of the same mountain, and the difference in flight period may be up to two weeks.

A general statement about distribution is given for each species. It would have been impossible to list all the states of the US in which each butterfly is found; all-embracing comments have been made instead. For instance, a species present in the southwestern deserts of the United States may be 'from Oregon, southeast to Colorado and New Mexico, and west to Baja California'.

All butterflies are reproduced life-size unless otherwise indicated.

SWALLOWTAILS

A group of relatively large and highly
mobile butterflies with bright colors.
These include not only the true swallowtails,
which have 'tails', but a group of mountain butterflies called parnassians and
apollos, which do not have tails. Several of
the North American swallowtails have
stronger populations south of the Mexican
border, and move northward into
southern states during
the spring and summer.

♂♀

♂

Artemisia/Old World Swallowtail

Papilio machaon

Identification   Two rows of medium-sized yellow patches running around margins and across upper wings, blue suffusion through dark band of hindwing, variable as subspecies.
Habitat   Waysides, clearings, tundra.
Flight period   One, June–July.
Distribution   Alaska to Lake Superior.

♂♀

♀

Western/Anise Swallowtail *Papilio zelicaon*

Identification   Female heavily marked in black and larger than male, black borders to forewings in both sexes, black toward base of forewing, and thick black border on hindwing, dusted with blue, yellow marks on forewing angled, underside hindwing with more blue dusting than uppers.
Habitat   Various, from urban areas to forest clearings.
Flight period   One in north, continuous in southwest.
Distribution   West coast of North America to Wyoming.

♂♀

♂

American/Eastern Black Swallowtail

Papilio polyxenes

Identification Row of yellow spots and yellow band across wings, with orange-red eye-spot, blue suffusion around hindwings more pronounced in female, orange background in east of range, yellow in west, variable as subspecies.
Habitat Flowery open areas and gardens.
Flight period Three, February–November.
Distribution From Manitoba to Maine, south to Florida and west to southern California.

♂♀

Short-tailed Swallowtail *Papilio brevicauda*

Identification   Named after its short, stunted tails, series of yellow dots and patches across wings, red-black eye-spots on hindwing, variable sizes, and variable as subspecies.
Habitat   Coastal gardens and hillsides.
Flight period   One, June–July.
Distribution   Eastern coast of Canada, Newfoundland, south Labrador.

♂♀

Cliff/Short-tailed Black Swallowtail

Papilio indra

Identification   Black abdomen with or without yellow dash by side of tip, black wings with large pale yellow markings crossing wings, variable as subspecies.
Habitat   Deserts, mountains, foothills, canyon cliffs.
Flight period   One–two northward.
Distribution   West coast United States, east to Wyoming.

90% life-size

♂♀

♀

Bahamas Swallowtail *Papilio andraemon*

Identification   Upper and lower wings with prominent broad orange band on black background.
Habitat   Gardens and waysides.
Flight period   April–October, as rare stray.
Distribution   Tip of Florida.

90% life-size

♂♀

♀

Giant/Orange Dog Swallowtail *Papilio cresphontes*

Identification   A large brown butterfly with yellow band
across uppers, female larger, and series of yellow spots round
wings, yellow on tail and toward tip of forewing, underside very
pale yellow throughout.
Habitat   Gardens, glades, roadsides, and citrus groves.
Flight period   Continuous in south, two toward north.
Distribution   Mostly east coast from New York to Florida,
and west to the Mississippi, occasionally even further westward
but not to coast.

♂♀

King/Thoas Swallowtail *Papilio thoas*

Identification   A large brown butterfly with one major yellow band crossing uppers, and series of yellow spots around edges, small reddish eye-spot on hindwing, three yellow squarish spots near leading edge of underside of forewing.

Habitat   Gardens, flowery glades, and waysides.

Flight period   Continuous, as stray.

Distribution   Arizona, New Mexico, Texas to Kansas.

♂♀

♂

Island/Schaus' Swallowtail *Papilio aristodemus*

Identification   Brown background color to uppers with crisp yellow bar across wings and yellow spots around edges, brown tail, reddish bar across underside of hindwing.
Habitat   Hammocks.   **Flight period**   April–June.
Distribution   South Florida islands.

♂

Ornythion Swallowtail *Papilio ornythion*

Identification   Broad yellow band across forewing with no yellow mark in forewing cell.
Habitat   Woods and citrus groves.
Flight period   Probably continuous in south Texas, strays elsewhere.
Distribution   Arizona, Texas, New Mexico.

♂♀

Red-spotted/Ruby-spotted Swallowtail

Papilio anchisiades

Identification   Black wings with rays of white on forewings, hindwing scalloped, no tails.
Habitat   Gardens and citrus groves.
Flight period   March–November.
Distribution   Texas as irregular stray and sometimes resident.

OPPOSITE

Astylus Swallowtail *Papilio astylus*

Identification   Broad yellow band, with yellow mark in forewing cell.
Habitat   Woods and citrus groves.
Flight period   Continuous in south Texas, strays elsewhere.
Distribution   Arizona and Texas.

90% life-size

♂♀

♂

Queen Swallowtail *Papilio androgeus*

Identification   Sexes completely different, male with very broad yellow band across wings, female with dark green bands across upper hindwing, uncluttered forewing and subsidiary tails, underside of male pale yellow with dark margins.
Habitat   Woods, gardens, and citrus groves.
Flight period   March–September.
Distribution   Southern tip of Florida.

♂♀

♀

Tiger Swallowtail *Papilio glaucus*

Identification   Black tiger stripes cross fore and hindwings in both sexes, black tails, light underside with black highlighted veins, females sometimes occur as a black form, variable as subspecies and forms.
Habitat   Gardens and waysides.
Flight period   March–November.
Distribution   Most of North America and Alaska, except within Arctic Circle.

♂♀

♀

Pale Tiger Swallowtail *Papilio eurymedon*

Identification   Mostly black markings with long streaks of pale yellow to white traversing wings, borders strongly black with minimum markings, more white dusting on underside, which has a repeat pattern of the uppers.

Habitat   Coast to chaparral and mountains.

Flight period   One, April–July.

Distribution   British Columbia to southern California to New Mexico.

95% life-size

Laurel/Palamedes Swallowtail

Papilio palamedes

Identification   Dart-shaped row of yellow spots crosses forewings, repeated on underside, hindwing underside with red darts in center and by margin.

Habitat Wetlands.   **Flight period**   February–December.

Distribution   Southeastern United States, especially Everglades.

Two-tailed Tiger Swallowtail

Papilio multicaudata

Identification   Named after the two unequal tails on each hindwing, dark margins with yellow spots, center of uppers yellow with one black streak crossing wings.
Habitat   Gardens, canyons, creeks, mountains.
Flight period   February–November.
Distribution   Western United States and southern British Columbia.

OPPOSITE

Spicebush Swallowtail *Papilio troilus*

Identification   Greenish-blue suffusion over most of uppersides of hindwing, two rows of red spots on hindwing, forewings dark with row of yellow spots around inside of margins.
Habitat   Gardens, woods, meadows, forests.
Flight period   April–October.
Distribution   East of the Mississippi.

Three-tailed Tiger Swallowtail *Papilio pilumnus*

Identification   Three tails on hindwing, one very long.
Habitat   Woodland.   **Flight period**   Spring–Fall.
Distribution   South Texas as rare stray.

♂♀

♀

Asian Swallowtail *Papilio xuthus*

Identification Black background, especially in female, with yellow banding across upper wings in male, blue suffusion of hindwing with eye-spot.
Habitat Woodlands and urban areas.
Flight period Continuous.
Distribution Hawaii as introduced species.

♂♀

90% life-size

Victorinus Swallowtail *Papilio victorinus*

Identification   Dark brown butterfly with two neat rows of yellow spots around uppers, on underside of hindwing rows are repeated in red.
Habitat   Woods and gardens.
Flight period   January–November.
Distribution   South Texas as stray.

♂♀

♀

Pipevine Swallowtail *Battus philenor*

Identification   Dark gray to black background color with suffusion of greenish hue on hindwing, and large orange spots on underside of hindwing.
Habitat   Waysides with pipevines and wild flowers, also gardens.
Flight period   Two–three, January–October.
Distribution   Principally southeast United States, venturing to west coast and north to Great Lakes.

♂♀

♀

Gold Rim/Polydamus Swallowtail

Battus polydamas

Identification   The 'gold rim' refers to the band of yellow-gold round margins of wings, no tail, and red rim to inside of margin of underside of hindwing.
Habitat   Agricultural areas and gardens.
Flight period   March–December.
Distribution   Southern Texas and Florida, with patchy distribution between the two states.

♂♀

♀

Zebra Swallowtail *Eurytides marcellus*

Identification   Long tails, though shorter in spring than summer, triangular wings with double pairs of tiger marks crossing light-colored wing.
Habitat   Waysides and meadows.
Flight period   March–December.
Distribution   Southeastern United States, north to New York.

Cuban Kite Swallowtail *Eurytides celadon*

Identification   Like *marcellus* but with less overall white and red marks on inside of hindwing.
Habitat   Waysides.   **Flight period**   Summer.
Distribution   South Florida as rare or doubtful stray.

Dark Kite/Dark Zebra Swallowtail

Eurytides philolaus

Identification   Long tails with broken red squiggle across underside of hindwing.
Habitat   Waysides.   **Flight period**   Summer.
Distribution   South Texas as rare stray.

Cattle Heart *Parides eurimedes*

Identification   Reddish band in center of hindwing, cream band in center of forewing.
Habitat   Waysides.   **Flight period**   Summer.
Distribution   South Texas as rare stray.

Yellow/Eversmann's Parnassian

Parnassius eversmanni

Identification   Males are yellow, females are white, both with considerable amounts of gray bands and bluish veins dispersed over wings, giving dusty appearance, red spot prominent.
Habitat   Tundra and mountains.
Flight period   One, June–July (two years to maturation).
Distribution   Alaska, Yukon, British Columbia, Northwest Territories.

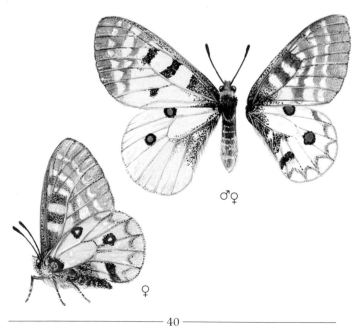

♂♀

♀

Small/Phoebus Parnassian *Parnassius phoebus*

Identification   Male whitish-cream with variable red spots on hindwings, female darker with transparent areas.
Habitat   Flowery sites with foodplant.
Flight period   One, June–September.
Distribution   Alaska to southern California and New Mexico.

OPPOSITE

American/Clodius Parnassian *Parnassius clodius*

Identification   Large rounded wings, cream with black and red spot in male, female white-gray wings and more dusty appearance on forewing, variable red spots on hindwing, female with waxy pouch on abdomen after mating.
Habitat   Coasts, canyons, and mountains.
Flight period   One, June–July.
Distribution   Southern California and Utah to Alaska.

WHITES AND SULPHURS

A very successful group of medium-sized butterflies which includes the familiar 'whites' of the garden, the orange tips of the wayside, and the yellows and sulphurs of mountain meadows. Members of this family exhibit different seasonal forms, as well as subspecies, which can hinder identification. Their caterpillars feed on a variety of plants belonging to the cabbage family, and some species are migratory.

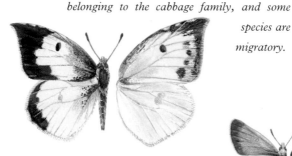

♂♀♀

Pine White *Neophasia menapia*

Identification   Male white with black tips interrupted with white marks, also gray veins to hindwing, female yellow background color, and margins of hindwing tinged in orange.
Habitat   Pine forests.   **Flight period**   July–September.
Distribution   British Columbia, west coast east to Dakota and south to New Mexico.

♂♀♀

Mexican Pine/Chiricahua Pine White

Neophasia terlootii

Identification   Sexes dissimilar, male with white background color, female orange, long black patch on forewing of both sexes, ring of red spots around underside of female hindwing.
Habitat   Pine forests.   **Flight period**   October–November.
Distribution   Mexico, Arizona.

$\male\female$

Nimbice White *Catasticta nimbice*

Identification   Brown background color with indented forewing and white band crossing wings, light spots to edge of forewings and scalloped pattern to edge of hindwing underside.
Habitat   Scrub, clearings.   **Flight period**   Spring.
Distribution   Mexico.

$\male\female\female$

Tropical/Florida White *Appias drusilla*

Identification   Forewing somewhat curved and pointed, male with very pale wings and black tip to forewing, female with bold black margins, underside gray-green with green at base of forewing, female variable in size and color.
Habitat   Mature hammocks.
Flight period   Continuous in southern Florida.
Distribution   Stray as far as Arizona and north to Iowa.

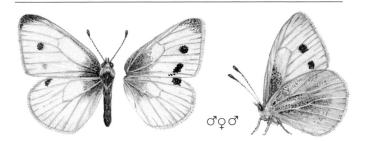

Cabbage Butterfly/Small White

Pieris rapae

Identification   Males with one black forewing spot, females with two, undersides yellow or greenish.
Habitat   Gardens, waysides, foothills.
Flight period   Three–four, March–November.
Distribution   All United States and southern Canada.

Sharp-veined/Veined White *Pieris napi*

Identification   Several forms, uppers white with black spots, paler in the summer, underside of hindwing with clear dark scales.
Habitat   Waysides, clearings, and damp meadows.
Flight period   Two–three, April–August.
Distribution   Alaska to Newfoundland; west coast and east to New Mexico.

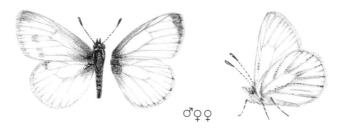

$\sigma \varphi \varphi$

Diffuse-veined/West Virginia White

Pieris virginiensis

Identification   Veins on underside of whitish hindwing are diffused with gray, male background color is white-gray, female pale yellow.
Habitat   Damp meadows and woodlands.
Flight period   One, April–May.
Distribution   Ontario to North Carolina in six states.

$\sigma \varphi$

Spring White *Pieris sisymbrii*

Identification   Both sexes with speckled black spots around margin and tip of forewing, gray veins on underside of hindwings.
Habitat   Lowlands to mountains.
Flight period   One, February–July.
Distribution   Yukon to Baja California and east to Dakota.

♂♀♀

Checkered White *Pieris protodice*

Identification   Dark checkering over white forewing of female, spring forms and those from high altitude are darker than summer and lowland specimens.
Habitat   Waysides and wastelands in lowlands.
Flight period   March–October.
Distribution   Almost all of United States and Mexico and southern Canada.

Great Basin White

Pieris chloridice

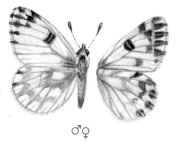

Identification   Dark veins on uppers and green veins on lowers.
Habitat   Foothills and deserts.
Flight period
March–October.
Distribution   Great Basin to Baja California, and east to Colorado.

♂♀

σ♀σ

Becker's White *Pieris chloridice beckerii*

Identification   White uppers, more speckled with black in female, underside of hindwing with radiating bands of mottled green, black mark on center of underside of forewing, subspecies of *P. chloridice*, also thought to have true species status.
Habitat   Foothills, canyons, mountains.
Flight period   Two, May–September.
Distribution   British Columbia to South Dakota and west to Baja California.

σ♀σ

Peak White *Pieris callidice*

Identification   Pale background color with small forewing marks in males and black forewing spots in female.
Habitat   Lowlands and mountains.
Flight period   One–two, May–July.
Distribution   Alaska to California and east to New Mexico.

♂♀

Western White *Pieris callidice occidentalis*

Identification   Checkered nature to wings, greenish scales over underside of hindwing, darker spring broods, subspecies of *P. callidice*, also thought to have true species status.
Habitat   Lowlands to mountains in Arctic.
Flight period   Two, April–September.
Distribution   Alaska to New Mexico.

♂♀

Southern/Great Southern White

Ascia monuste

Identification   Male whitish-green uppers with scalloped black marginal marks on upper forewing, more pronounced in female which has pale orange background color, female gray all over, or like male, variable as subspecies.
Habitat   Coastal habitats migrating inland.
Flight period   Continuous in south.
Distribution   A tropical species which occurs in the south of Baja California, Mexico, southern Texas, southern Florida.

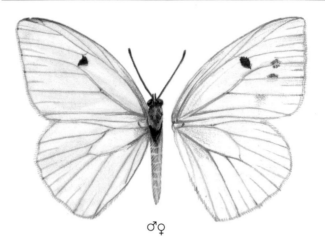

Giant White *Ascia josephina*

Identification   A relatively large butterfly, male with greenish hue, female cream, both with black spot on pointed forewing.
Habitat   Scrubby areas.   **Flight period**   Continuous.
Distribution   Mexico and southern tip of Texas.

Dappled Marble/Creamy Marblewing

Euchloe ausonia

Identification   White-cream uppers with more extensive black markings on forewing tip of female than male, underside of hindwing mottled with network of green scales.
Habitat   Clearings, meadows, lowlands.
Flight period   One–Two, February–August.
Distribution   Alaska to Ontario to New Mexico and California.

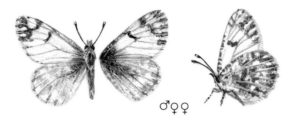

♂♀♀

Northern Marble/Northern Marblewing

Euchloe creusa

Identification   White-cream uppers, mottled forewing tips, extensive green mottling on underside of hindwing visible on uppers.
Habitat   Alpine meadows and moraines.
Flight period   One, May–July.
Distribution   Alaska to south of British Columbia.

♂♀♀

Rosy Marble/Olympia Marblewing

Euchloe olympia

Identification   Named after the rosy tint to undersides of green-mottled hindwing, uppers very pale.
Habitat   Meadows, clearings, foothills, and dunes.
Flight period   One, March–June.
Distribution   Central United States and east into Virginia.

Western Marble/ Pearly Marblewing

Euchloe hyantis

♂♀

Identification   Uppers greenish-white, with black mottled forewing tips, broad bands of dark green on underside of hindwing, pearly sheen, variable as subspecies.
Habitat   Woodland, chaparral, desert.
Flight period   One, February–May.
Distribution   South of British Columbia to Mexico and Baja California.

Desert Orange Tip

Anthocharis cethura

♂♀

Identification   Orange 'tips' are to inside of black tips, white marks are dispersed in the black tips of female, green markings on underside of hindwing as loose bands, variable as subspecies.
Habitat   Desert and chaparral.
Flight period   One, February–May.
Distribution   California to New Mexico.

♂♀♀

Pima Orange Tip *Anthocharis cethura pima*

Identification   Bright yellow background color to wings of both sexes, subspecies of *P. cethura*, also regarded as true species status.
Habitat   Foothills, canyons, and desert.
Flight period   One, February–April.
Distribution   Sonoran desert in southwestern United States.

♂♀♂

Western/Sara Orange Tip *Anthocharis sara*

Identification   Male either white or yellow, female deep yellow, red-orange tip on forewing to inside of black tip of female, underside mottled green.
Habitat   Meadows, clearings, waysides.
Flight period   February–July.
Distribution   British Columbia to Mexico and New Mexico.

Falcate Orange Tip

Anthocharis midea

♂♀

Identification
Characteristic hooked forewing, delicate mottled patterning on underside of hindwing, only male has orange tip.
Habitat   Waysides, clearings, and meadows.
Flight period   April–May.
Distribution   East of the Mississippi north to Great Lakes and south to Georgia.

California White Tip/Gray Marble

Anthocharis lanceolata

♂♀

Identification   White-greenish background color and stubby-shaped forewing, black dashing around upperside margins, undersides with brown peppering.
Habitat   Meadows, waysides, canyons.
Flight period   One, March–May.
Distribution   Oregon to northern Baja California.

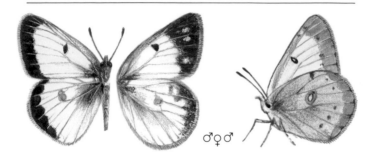

Common Sulphur *Colias philodice*

Identification   Uppers yellow with dark bands, white female forms, pale yellow patches in dark marginal band of female, orange spot in center of upper hindwing, variable as subspecies.
Habitat   Meadows, forests, deserts.
Flight period   Two or three, March–December.
Distribution   Alaska to Great Lakes and Newfoundland, most of United States, except tip of Florida and Californian coast.

Alfalfa/Orange Sulphur *Colias eurytheme*

Identification   Deep orange-red uppers, more subdued in female, which has yellow mottles in black border, lemon-yellow underside hindwing, variable as forms.
Habitat   Almost ubiquitous.
Flight period   Continuous, March–December.
Distribution   Most of United States, except west coast and southeast, Canada from Alaska to Ontario.

Ultraviolet/Queen Alexandra's Sulphur

Colias alexandra

Identification Male citron-yellow with black borders and yellow veins, female with more strident colors, variable as subspecies.
Habitat Waysides, meadows, sagelands.
Flight period One, June–July.
Distribution Rocky Mountains and Great Plains.

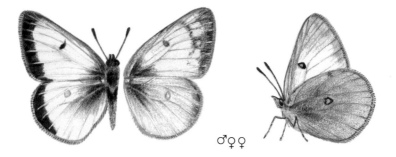

♂♀

♂♀♀

Golden Sulphur/Western Sulphur

Colias occidentalis

Identification Male citron-yellow and dark margins, female pale yellow with gray toward tip of forewing, pink fringes to wings and pink legs, underside dirty gray-yellow.
Habitat Coastal, meadows, and clearings.
Flight period One, June–August.
Distribution British Columbia to California.

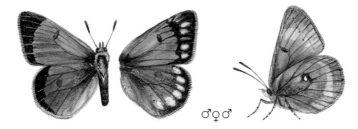

Alpine Orange/Mead's Sulphur *Colias meadii*

Identification   Thick brown bands on margins of orange
wings, distinctive dark green suffusion to undersides of
hindwing and especially on margin of forewing, variable as
subspecies.
Habitat   Tundra, streams, and rocky slopes.
Flight period   One, July–August.
Distribution   Isolated populations from British Columbia to
northern New Mexico.

Arctic Orange/Greenland Sulphur

Colias hecla

Identification   Dark underside of hindwing, dark margin of
upper forewing with dark veins, female white with dark shading.
Habitat   Alpine pastures.
Flight period   One, June–August.
Distribution   Alaska to Greenland in high Arctic.

Arctic Green/Labrador Sulphur

Colias nastes

Identification Small and much suffused, with dark red edge of forewing, variable as subspecies.
Habitat Barren tundra.
Flight period One, July–August.
Distribution Alaska south to Montana, and east to Newfoundland.

♂♀

Thula Sulphur

Colias nastes thula

Identification Greenish tinge to uppers and narrow forewing borders, subspecies of *C. nastes*, and also thought to have true species status.
Habitat Tundra.
Flight period Undescribed.
Distribution Alaska.

♂

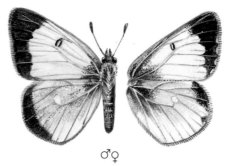

♂♀

Arctic/Palaeno Sulphur *Colias palaeno*

Identification Yellow spot in center of forewing, female sometimes white.
Habitat Tundra and taiga.
Flight period One, June–August.
Distribution Alaska to Hudson Bay.

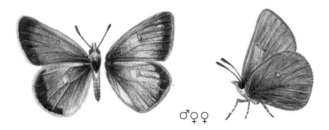

$\male \female \female$

Sierra Green/Behr's Sulphur *Colias behrii*

Identification   Male green-yellow uppers with dark margins,
female dirty cream uppers, green suffusion over undersides,
pink suffusion around wings.
Habitat   Mountain meadows.
Flight period   One, July–September.
Distribution   Yosemite National Park.

$\male \female$

Pink-edged Sulphur

Colias interior

Identification   Pronounced
pink fringes around wings,
and red ring around central
hindwing spot.
Habitat   Meadows,
waysides, and bogs.
Flight period   One,
June–August.
Distribution   A broad band
from Oregon to
Newfoundland.

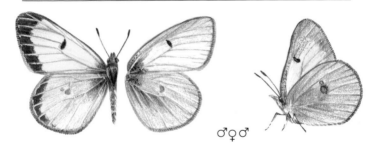

♂♀♂

Blueberry Sulphur *Colias pelidne*

Identification   Male lemon-yellow, female pale yellow or white, both with pink fringes and pink legs, variable as subspecies.
Habitat   Tundra, mountains, huckleberry heaths.
Flight period   July and August.
Distribution   Scattered in three areas centered on Idaho, Yukon, and Quebec.

Willow/Scudder's Willow Sulphur

Colias scudderi

♂♀

Identification   Male yellow uppers with black margins, female greenish tips and pink margins, greenish tinge below, variable as subspecies.
Habitat   Bogs and meadows.
Flight period   One, June–August.
Distribution   Alaska to south of Hudson Bay, with scattered localities from British Columbia to New Mexico.

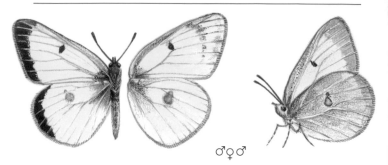

Great Northern Sulphur

Colias scudderi gigantea

Identification   Relatively large butterfly, lemon-yellow and black margins in male, pink fringes, subspecies of *C. scudderi*, also thought to have true species status.
Habitat   Bogs and taiga.   **Flight period**   One, June–August.
Distribution   Yukon to Manitoba.

Dog Face/Dogface Butterfly   *Colias cesonia*

Identification   Characteristic yellow 'dog face' in thick dark margin of both sexes, less pronounced in female.
Habitat   Woodlands, scrub, desert.
Flight period   Continuous in south, June–August elsewhere.
Distribution   Based in south from Baja California and Mexico to Florida, with migration north to Great Lakes.

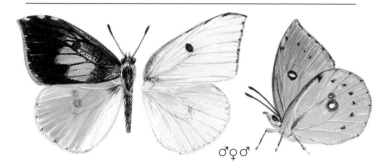

♂♀♂

California Dogface *Colias eurydice*

Identification   Pointed forewing, male with 'dog face' shot with a purple tinge, absent in female, which has a single black spot on forewing.
Habitat   Foothills, clearings.
Flight period   Two, March–September.
Distribution   Northern California to Baja in coastal ranges.

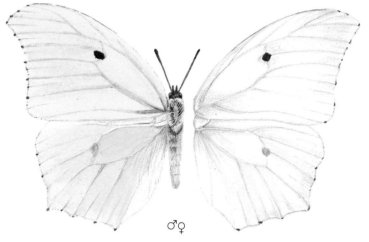

♂♀

Yellow Brimstone/Yellow Angled Sulphur

Anteos maerula

Identification   Male bright yellow, female cream yellow, both with black forewing spot, and orange hindwing spot, dusky green-yellow below.
Habitat   Woods.   **Flight period**   Continuous.
Distribution   Mexico, as rare stray to southeast States.

♂♀

♀

Ghost Brimstone/White Angled Sulphur

Anteos clorinde

Identification   A large greenish butterfly, hooked forewing with strong yellow patch, underside darker green, female with large black dot in each wing ringed in orange.
Habitat   Scrub and clearings.
Flight period   One, July–October.
Distribution   Mexico, penetrating to Colorado.

σ♀σ

Cloudless Giant Sulphur *Phoebis sennae*

Identification   Male bright yellow, female pale cream with dark margin, underside lemon with reddish cloudy marks.
Habitat   Gardens, waysides, meadows, and coasts.
Flight period   Continuous in south, two toward north.
Distribution   Mexico and southern Florida, reaching north to Great Lakes.

σ♀

Apricot Sulphur/Argante Giant Sulphur
Phoebis argante

Identification   Male rich orange uppers with a few marginal black marks, female dull yellow with larger marginal marks and main spots.
Habitat   Scrubby areas.   **Flight period**   Continuous.
Distribution   Mexico, straying north to Kansas.

♂♀

♀

Orange-barred Giant Sulphur *Phoebis philea*

Identification   Male yellow with pale orange bar in forewing and orange suffusion over yellow hindwing, female dusky pink with dark margins, undersides suffused with reddish waves, dark margin.
Habitat   Gardens, scrub.   **Flight period**   Continuous.
Distribution   Southern Florida, reaching as far north as Great Lakes and west to Arizona.

♂♀

Large Orange/ Orange Giant Sulphur

♀

Phoebis agarithe

Identification   Male deep orange uppers, female orange or white, undersides dirty speckled reddish-yellow.
Habitat   Clearings and scrub.
Flight period   Continuous, March–December.
Distribution   Southwest Mexico penetrating north to Great Lakes; southern Florida.

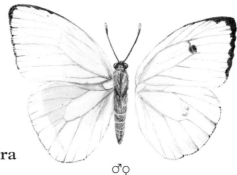

Migrant Sulphur/Statira

Phoebis statira

♂♀

Identification   Male with bright yellow bases to wings, female yellow with dark margin to forewing uppers, pink antennae.
Habitat   Coastal.   **Flight period**   Two, February–June.
Distribution   Southern Florida and Mexico, venturing north to southern Texas.

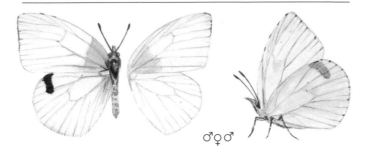

♂♀♂

Guayacan Sulphur/Lyside *Kricognia lyside*

Identification   Male white or greenish-yellow, female pale yellow, form terissa with black bar, underside pale yellow, extremely variable.
Habitat   Plains.   **Flight period**   Continuous.
Distribution   Mexico, Arizona, Texas to Nebraska.

♂♀♂

Tailed Orange *Eurema proterpia*

Identification   The only *Eurema* with tails but they are sometimes absent, dark margins to forewings, and black veins in summer forms.
Habitat   Open scrub.
Flight period   Three, July–October.
Distribution   Mexico, Arizona, New Mexico, Texas to Nebraska.

Little Sulphur/ Little Yellow

Eurema lisa

♂♀

Identification A little butterfly, both sexes yellow, female sometimes white or pale yellow, both with black tip to forewing.
Habitat Waysides and meadows.
Flight period Continuous, May–October to the north.
Distribution Southwestern states, venturing north to Great Lakes and west to Mexico.

Blacktip Sulphur/ Mimosa Yellow

Eurema nise

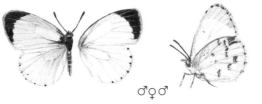

♂♀♂

Identification A small butterfly with bold black tips to forewings of both sexes and tiny dots on hindwing edge, mottled underside of hindwing.
Habitat Waysides. **Flight period** Continuous.
Distribution Mexico and north into southern United States, and in south of Florida.

Rambling Orange/ Sleepy Orange

Eurema nicippe

♂♀

Identification Broad black borders to orange wings, underside pale yellow with dirty speckling.
Habitat Woods, meadows, canyons.
Flight period Continuous, March–November northward.
Distribution Across southern United States and Mexico, venturing north to Great Lakes.

♂♀♀

Poodle-face Sulphur/Boisduval's Yellow

Eurema boisduvaliana

Identification   Male with poodle-shaped yellow mark highlighted in black margin, female with a simple black tip to forewing.
Habitat   Scrub and clearings.   **Flight period**   Continuous.
Distribution   Mexico, Arizona, New Mexico, Texas, southern Florida.

Wolf-face Sulphur/Mexican Yellow

Eurema mexicana

♂♀

Identification   Wolf-face pattern etched in white on dark forewing tip, orange on forward edge of upper hindwing of male, female palest lemon wings.
Habitat   Meadows, chaparral, canyons.
Flight period March–November.
Distribution   Mexico, Arizona, and New Mexico, and as migrants as far north as Manitoba.

Dainty Sulphur/Dwarf Yellow

Nathalis iole

♂♀♀

Identification   Tiny (the tiniest pierid in North America), female forewing black at tip against yellow background color, undersides of male smoky or yellowish and with three black dots.
Habitat   Waysides, canyons.   **Flight period**   Continuous.
Distribution   Baja California to Florida and all southern states, northward as migrant to Manitoba.

BRUSH-FOOTED BUTTERFLIES

A large family of butterflies which includes several allies, such as the aristocrats (with aristocratic colors and names), fritillaries, browns, danaids, and the snouts. All of them have four functional legs, a feature which separates them from some other families which have six. Mostly powerful fliers and colonizers of all sorts of habitats, several of the brush-footed butterflies are strongly migratory, especially the monarch.

Aristocrats

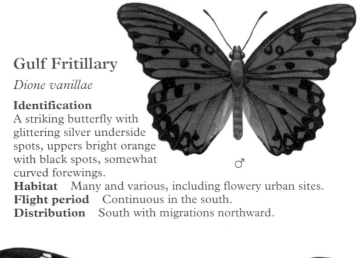

Gulf Fritillary

Dione vanillae

Identification
A striking butterfly with glittering silver underside spots, uppers bright orange with black spots, somewhat curved forewings.

♂

Habitat   Many and various, including flowery urban sites.
Flight period   Continuous in the south.
Distribution   South with migrations northward.

♂♀

Zebra Longwing *Heliconius charitonia*

Identification   Long wings-to-body ratio, zebra-like markings on both surfaces but of alternating yellow and brown colors, pale cream on undersides, red dot at base of hindwings.
Habitat   Woodland edges, hammocks.
Flight period   Continuous in the south; one, April–November in Texas.
Distribution   Southern states.

Variegated Fritillary

♀ *Euptoieta claudia*

Identification   Larger female. Soft orange colors interspersed with lines and dots of black on uppers, underside hindwing pattern unique, with rich orange at base of forewing.
Habitat   Meadows and other grassy areas.
Flight period   Continuous in south; one, March–December northward.
Distribution   Southern states, reaching into Canada.

Aphrodite Fritillary

Speyeria

aphrodite

Identification
Female larger with rounder forewing tips, orange uppers speckled with black marks, underside forewing pattern reversal of uppers, hindwing rufous and covered with white spots.
Habitat   Woods and wet meadows.
Flight period
One, June–September.
Distribution   Almost east to west in United States and Canada, but blocked by Rockies.

♂♀

♂

♂♀

♀

Great Smokies/Diana Fritillary *Speyeria diana*

Identification Sexes completely different, female blue with black uppers, male dark brown with striking orange marginal band, dark mottled underside.
Habitat Woodlands, meadows, and glades.
Flight period One, June–September.
Distribution Louisiana to Maryland.

♂♀

Great Spangled Fritillary *Speyeria cybele*

Identification   Female slightly larger than male, with large silver spangles on underside of hindwing, uppers orange with black marks darker toward the base, variable as subspecies.
Habitat   Meadows and woodland glades.
Flight period   One, June–September.
Distribution   East to west coasts of United States, southern Canada.

♂♀

♀

Regal Fritillary *Speyeria idalia*

Identification   Female larger and darker than male, dark margins of wings, with liberal amounts of pale yellow spots on underside hindwing.
Habitat   Wet meadows.
Flight period   One, June–September.
Distribution   Central United States to east coast.

♂♀

Western Seep/Nokomis Fritillary

Speyeria nokomis

Identification   Female is slightly larger than male and is pale yellow with black marks, round wingtips, underside of female has a fuscous forewing underside, underside hindwing is pale brown in male, dark in female, variable as subspecies.
Habitat   Named after its habitat: wet meadows – seeps.
Flight period   One, July–September.
Distribution   Disjointed distribution in southwestern United States, and southward.

♂♀♂

Coronis Fritillary *Speyeria coronis*

Identification   String of flattened silver marks around margin of underside hindwing is characteristic, while rest of hindwing has other silver marks, uppers orange with black marks, variable as subspecies.
Habitat   Chaparral.   **Flight period**   One, June–September.
Distribution   Western to central United States.

Green/Edward's Fritillary
♀ *Speyeria edwardsii*

Identification   Greenish tinge to underside hindwing, which is covered in silver spots, uppers orange with dark markings.
Habitat   Prairie and chaparral.
Flight period   One, June–September.
Distribution   Alberta to Manitoba, south to New Mexico.

♂♀

Zerene Fritillary *Speyeria zerene*

Identification   Female larger than male, black spots and lines on uppers, underside hindwing speckled with silver spots, variable with many subspecies.
Habitat   Dunes, meadows, waysides.
Flight period   One, June–September.
Distribution   British Columbia to California, east to Dakota.

Callippe Fritillary *Speyeria callippe*

Identification   Orange uppers with black marks, including zig-zag ones on hindwing, underside with greenish hue surrounding silver spots, variable as subspecies.
Habitat   Grassy open woodlands and chaparral.
Flight period   One, June–August.
Distribution   Northwestern United States and southeastern Canada.

Great Basin/ Egleis Fritillary

Speyeria egleis

Identification   Uppers heavily marked in typical dark pattern, underside of hindwing suffused in green, variable as subspecies.
Habitat Woodland clearings.
Flight period One, June–August.
Distribution Washington state to California, east to Colorado.

♂♀♂

Atlantis Fritillary *Speyeria atlantis*

Identification Orange uppers, paler in female, with series of chevrons, bars, and spots, pattern repeated on underside forewing, silver spots set in brownish underside hindwing, variable as numerous subspecies.
Habitat Clearings and wet meadows.
Flight period One, July–August.
Distribution Alaska to Newfoundland and south to Arizona.

♂♀♂

Lavender/Hydaspe Fritillary *Speyeria hydaspe*

Identification Named after pale lavender color to underside hindwings, which are dominantly reddish-brown in hue, variable as subspecies.
Habitat Woodland clearings.
Flight period One, July–August.
Distribution British Columbia to California, east to Colorado.

♂♀♀

Mormon Fritillary *Speyeria mormonia*

Identification   Orange uppers with black marks, slightly darker to bases of wings, underside hindwing with silver spots.
Habitat   Lowland and alpine meadows.
Flight period   One, July–September.
Distribution   Alaska to California and New Mexico.

Ocellate/Bog Fritillary *Proclossiana eunomia*

♂♀

Identification   Orange uppers with dark spots, underside hindwing with uniform bands of spots and colors, variable as subspecies.
Habitat   Bogs.
Flight period   One, June–August.
Distribution   Mainly Alaska to Newfoundland.

Purple Bog/Titania's Fritillary *Clossiana titania*

♂♀

Identification   Underside of hindwing, which is dark, often with various white chevrons, has characteristic ring of white spots, variable as subspecies.
Habitat   Alpine meadows, bogs, tundra.
Flight period   One, June–August.
Distribution   Canada, south to New Mexico, Greenland coast.

$\male\female\male$

Arctic Fritillary *Clossiana chariclea*

Identification   Female slightly darker than male, underside
hindwing has four or more silver spots, also regarded as
subspecies of *C. titania*.
Habitat   Alpine meadows, bogs, tundra.
Flight period One, June–August. **Distribution** Arctic regions.

$\male\female\male$

Freya's Fritillary *Clossiana freija*

Identification   Underside of hindwing has several large
dashes which reach margin, while underside of forewing is rich
orange toward base.
Habitat   Tundra and bogs.   **Flight period**   One, May–July.
Distribution   Alaska to Newfoundland.

Polar Fritillary

Clossiana polaris

$\male\female$

Identification   Undersides
distinctive, with white marks
reaching margin from
marginal spots, uppers
chestnut with black lines.
Habitat   Tundra.
Flight period   One,
June–August.
Distribution   Alaska to
northern fringe of Greenland,
south into British Columbia.

Willow-bog/Frigga's Fritillary *Clossiana frigga*

Identification   Chestnut hindwing underside with rows of dark marks, lighter toward leading edge, orange uppers heavily marked to base of wing, variable as subspecies.
Habitat   Bogs.   **Flight period**   One, June–July.
Distribution   Alaska to Quebec and south into United States.

Dingy Arctic Fritillary *Clossiana improba*

Identification   Uppers with blurry black markings against palest background color, variable as subspecies.
Habitat   Arctic scrub and tundra.
Flight period   One, July–August.
Distribution   Alaska, North West Territories, south to Alberta.

Mountain/Napaea Fritillary *Boloria napaea*

Identification   Dark suffusion at base of orange uppers but mainly on hindwing, female with more subdued colors, variable as subspecies.
Habitat   Alpine meadows and tundra.
Flight period   One, July–August.
Distribution   Alaska south to Alberta.

Silver Meadow/Silver-bordered Fritillary

Boloria selene

Identification   Row of seven pearls ring margin of underside hindwing, otherwise a small butterfly with black marks on rich orange wings, variable as subspecies.
Habitat   Meadows, waysides, and clearings.
Flight period   Three, May–October.
Distribution   Alaska to Newfoundland, south to New Mexico.

Meadow Fritillary *Boloria bellona*

Identification   Forewing tip slightly indented in male, otherwise dark orange-brown wings and lack of any highlighting on hindwing, variable as subspecies.
Habitat   Meadows and pastures.
Flight period   Three, May–September.
Distribution   Yukon to Quebec, southeast to Georgia.

Relic Meadow/Kriemhild Fritillary

Boloria kriemhild

Identification   Disjointed band of brown-yellow crosses underside of hindwing, uppers orange with dark marks, and row of black spots around inside of margins.
Habitat   Meadows and clearings.
Flight period   One, June–August.
Distribution   Montana to Utah.

♂♀♂

Western Meadow Fritillary *Boloria epithore*

Identification   Uppers orange with black marks and flush of
lavender toward margins, underside of hindwing includes
yellow-brown band, variable as subspecies.
Habitat   Meadows and clearings.
Flight period   One, May–August.
Distribution   British Columbia to California.

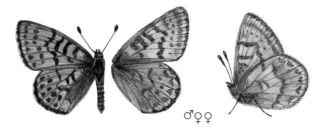

♂♀♀

Alberta Alpine Fritillary *Boloria alberta*

Identification   Male uppers a dingy color, female
considerably more dusky, muted gray and orange pattern,
underside a repeat of upper pattern.
Habitat   Alpine meadows.
Flight period   One, July–August.
Distribution   Alberta, British Columbia, Montana.

Pleistocene Fritillary

Boloria natazhati

♂♀

Identification A small butterfly, overall dark and somber, female more so, dark bases to wings, otherwise orange and black patterns toward tips and on underside.
Habitat Mountains, scree.
Flight period One, June–July.
Distribution Alaska, Yukon, North West Territories, Victoria Island.

Arctic Ridge/ Astarte Fritillary

♂♀♂

Boloria astarte

Identification Underside hindwing with silvery-gray band edged in black, background color orange, males with pointed forewings, variable as subspecies.
Habitat Rocky arctic areas. **Flight period** One, June–August.
Distribution Alaska to Washington state.

Texas Crescent/ Texas Crescentspot

♂♂

Phyciodes texana

Identification Dark uppers with white spots on forewing, orange toward base, hindwing with white bar crossing wing, underside of hindwing pale, variable as subspecies.
Habitat Desert, grasslands, scrub.
Flight period Continuous in south, otherwise March–November.
Distribution Southern states, with few exceptions.

♂♀♀

Mat-plant/Phaon Crescentspot *Phyciodes phaon*

Identification Sexes fairly similar with dark margins, more orange on female upper hindwing than male, black spot on hindwing, underside hindwing light and yellow with convoluted pattern, base of underside of forewing orange.
Habitat Creeks, springs, and damp fields.
Flight period Two, April–September.
Distribution All southern states, southward.

Pearl/Pearly Crescentspot

Phyciodes tharos

♂♀

Identification Uppers very orangey with dark margins around all wings, hindwing has rows of orange spots and white lunules.
Habitat Meadows, fields, prairie.
Flight period Several, April–August.
Distribution Alberta to Maine, and across United States to Arizona.

Dark Crescent/ Tawny Crescentspot

♂♀♀

Phyciodes batesii

Identification Both sexes very dark, especially around margins of uppers, female slightly larger, undersides light tan with whitish row of spots around margin.
Habitat Meadows, fields, waysides.
Flight period Several, April–November.
Distribution North West Territories to Nova Scotia.

♂♀ ♀

Field Crescent/Crescentspot *Phyciodes campestris*

Identification   Female slightly larger, speckled with two-tone colors on uppers, orange and yellow-orange, underside of hindwing pale tan, pale orange on underside of forewing, variable as subspecies.
Habitat   Meadows, fields, clearings.
Flight period   Four, April–October.
Distribution   Alaska to New Mexico.

Painted Crescent/ Crescentspot

Phyciodes picta

♂♀

Identification   Very small with muted dark brown uppers, underside hindwing yellow and unmarked in male, cream in female.
Habitat   Flowery waysides and disturbed ground.
Flight period   Two, May–August.
Distribution   Nebraska, southward.

♂♀ ♀

Mesquite Crescent/Crescentspot

Phyciodes vesta

Identification   Dark uppers with light orange marks, and orange and yellow markings below in tight lines and rows.
Habitat   Grassy areas and deserts.
Flight period   Continuous, April–October.
Distribution   Nebraska, southward.

Pale Crescent/ Pallid Crescentspot

Phyciodes pallida

Identification   Light brown uppers uncluttered with lots of black marks, female slightly larger, somewhat faded look, with slightly sculptured margins and indented forewing.
Habitat   Foothills, canyons, washes.
Flight period   One, April–June.
Distribution   British Columbia to New Mexico.

Thistle Crescent/ Mylitta Crescentspot

Phyciodes mylitta

Identification   Small with very light orange uppers and black marks darker in female, forewing slightly indented, variable as subspecies.
Habitat   Meadows, fields, waysides.
Flight period   Several, March–October.
Distribution   Southern Canada and most of western United States down to Mexico.

Great Plains/ Gorgone Checkerspot

Chlosyne gorgone

Identification   Bright orange yellow and brown uppers, underside hindwing gray with pronounced black marks across wing. Variable as forms.
Habitat   Flowery meadows and waysides.
Flight period   One, May–September.
Distribution   Alberta to Texas and Georgia.

Streamside/ Silvery Checkerspot

Chlosyne nycteis

Identification Uppers dark brown with orange and yellow marks, underside with yellow, orange and whitish marks by margin, variable as subspecies.
Habitat Meadows and woods.
Flight period Several, March–September.
Distribution Southern Canada and most of southeastern United States.

Eastern/Harris' Checkerspot *Chlosyne harrisii*

Identification Mostly dark uppers with dark margins all round, with bands of orange, variable as subspecies.
Habitat Meadows and waysides.
Flight period One, June–July.
Distribution North as well as east: Saskatchewan to Newfoundland.

Creamy/Northern Checkerspot *Chlosyne palla*

Identification Female with dark brown background color, male bright orange with black marks, female with pale cream spots, male with rich orange spots, variable as subspecies.
Habitat Chaparral, clearings.
Flight period One, May–July.
Distribution British Columbia to California.

Pearly/Gabb's Checkerspot *Chlosyne gabbii*

Identification   Color highly variable between subspecies, generally range from pallid yellow to orange uppers crossed by rows of dark marks, underside hindwing with plenty of white bands crossing wing.
Habitat   Alpine meadows, waysides.
Flight period   One, May–August.
Distribution   Saskatchewan to New Mexico.

Rockslide Checkerspot *Chlosyne gabbii damoestas*

Identification   Uppers suffused with dark brown or black, subspecies of *C. gabbii*.
Habitat   Alpine meadows, waysides.
Flight period   One, May–August.
Distribution   British Columbia, Alberta.

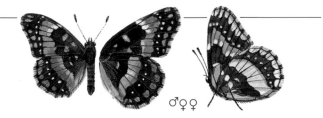

California Patch *Chlosyne californica*

Identification   Uppers with broad orange-brown band and chains of spots over brown background color, underside uncluttered with spots, with cream and orange bands and yellow-cream marginal spots against a light brown background.
Habitat   Canyons, hills.
Flight period   Several, March–November.
Distribution   Nevada to Baja California.

Sunflower/ Bordered Patch

Chlosyne lacinia

Identification   Uppers mostly brown with orange-white band across all wings, two rows of spots of white inside wings, highly variable as subspecies.
Habitat   Fields, woods, gardens.
Flight period   Several, March–November.
Distribution   Nevada, southward and east to New Mexico.

Paintbrush/ Leanira Checkerspot

Chlosyne leanira

Identification   Female very slightly larger than male, uppers of female slightly cloudy, on hindwing veins highlighted in black on both sides, underside of forewing chestnut with cream, variable as subspecies.
Habitat Prairies, foothills.   **Flight period** One, April–October.
Distribution   California to Colorado.

Mexican/ Theona Checkerspot

Chlosyne theona

Identification Female larger than male, both with prominent chain of white-cream and orange marks and spots crossing underside of hindwing and upper hindwing, variable as subspecies.
Habitat Forests, foothills, canyons.
Flight period Continuous, April–October.
Distribution Arizona to Texas, southward.

Small/Elada Checkerspot

Texola elada

Identification A small butterfly, uppers dark with orange background color, pattern crowded with at least three bands of orange and white marks on underside of hindwing.
Habitat Flowery meadows.
Flight period Continuous, April–October.
Distribution Arizona to Texas, southward.

Dotted Checkerspot

Poladryas minuta

Identification Uppers pale orange with numerous lines of black, indented forewing, underside of hindwing distinctive with two rows of black dashes crossing center of wing, and black marks around margin, variable as subspecies.
Habitat Flowery meadows, hilltops.
Flight period Continuous, January–September.
Distribution Wyoming south to Mexico.

Baltimore

Euphydryas phaeton

♂♀

Identification Dark uppers with distinctive orange marginal marks following inside with rows of palest yellow spots, more enlarged in female, female larger than male, upper pattern repeated more strongly on underside, more orange spots toward base of wings, variable as subspecies.
Habitat Meadows, bogs.
Flight period One, May–June.
Distribution East of Mississippi River.

♂♀♀

Western/Chalcedon Checkerspot

Euphydryas chalcedona

Identification Dark brown and cream uppers like a checkerboard, with a tinge of red-orange, below red-orange with cream and reddish marginal marks, highly variable as subspecies.
Habitat Desert, chaparral, clearings.
Flight period Several, April–October.
Distribution British Columbia to Baja California.

Ridge/Edith's Checkerspot

Euphydryas editha

Identification Uppers variable, either orange, yellow-orange, or red-orange with black marks, underside with whitish spots, variable as subspecies.
Habitat Grasslands, chaparral, tundra.
Flight period One, March–August.
Distribution British Columbia to California.

♂♀

♂♀

Question Mark *Polygonia interrogationis*

Identification Key features are long 'tail' on hindwing and white dot by silver question-mark on underside of hindwing, hindwing very much darker to outside, variable as forms.
Habitat Waysides and woodlands.
Flight period Continuous, May–September.
Distribution Saskatchewan to Arizona, eastward.

Comma Anglewing *Polygonia comma*

Identification   Outline of wings highly indented, undersides brown, short tail, reddish-brown above with black marks, variable as forms.
Habitat   Waysides and clearings.
Flight period   Three, March–October.
Distribution   Saskatchewan to Texas, eastward.

Golden/Satyr Anglewing *Polygonia satyrus*

Identification   Golden-brown uppers and rich brown hindwing underside, otherwise typical ragged outline of wing.
Habitat   Waysides, woodlands, foothills, urban.
Flight period   Three, February–September.
Distribution   Yukon to Newfoundland, south to Mexico.

♂♀♀

Hoary Comma/Hoary Anglewing
Polygonia gracilis

Identification   Orange ground color with darker margins, light yellow marks inside margins, light outer part to hindwing with touch of green and darker at base, variable as subspecies, or possibly true species status.
Habitat   Clearings, mountains.
Flight period   One, July as hibernator.
Distribution   Alaska to New England.

♂♀♂

Zephyr Anglewing *Polygonia gracilis zephyrus*

Identification   Pale suffusion on inside of dark margins, underside dark gray, lighter to outside, subspecies of *P. gracilis*, or possibly true species status.
Habitat   Waysides, forests, streamsides.
Flight period   Two, March–October.
Distribution   British Columbia to California and New Mexico.

Dark-gray Comma/ Anglewing

Polygonia progne

♂♀

Identification Hindwing uppers have a faint ring of yellow spots, and 2–3 black marks near base, female larger, undersides dark-gray, very slightly lighter toward margins, variable as subspecies.
Habitat Woods and forests.
Flight period One, July as hibernator.
Distribution California to Newfoundland, south to Oklahoma.

Oreas Anglewing

Polygonia progne oreas

♂♀

Identification Dark wedges traverse uppers midway between lighter marginal area and somber-colored base, subspecies of *P. progne*, or possibly true species status.
Habitat Streamsides, clearings, meadows.
Flight period One, July as hibernator.
Distribution British Columbia to California.

Green Comma/Faunus Anglewing

Polygonia faunus

Identification   Very dark undersides, pronounced ragged outline, green spots by margin on underside of hindwing sometimes present, variable as subspecies.
Habitat   Waysides, streamsides.
Flight period   One, June as hibernator.
Distribution   Alaska to Newfoundland, south to California and Georgia.

Hylas Comma/Colorado Anglewing

Polygonia faunus hylas

Identification   Orange ground color with black spots, distinct row of cream spots inside margins, dark underside with faint purple tinge, subspecies of *P. faunus*, or possibly separate species status.
Habitat   Streams, valleys.
Flight period   One, April–September.
Distribution   Arizona to Wyoming and New Mexico.

Silvius Comma

Polygonia faunus silvius   ♂♀

Identification   A relatively large butterfly, especially the
female, light yellow inside dark border, more orange on uppers
of female, subspecies of *P. faunus*, or possibly true species status.
Habitat   Streams, foothills.
Flight period   One, March–October.
Distribution   California.

♂♀

Comma/Compton Tortoiseshell

♂ *Nymphalis vau-album*

Identification   A striking comma, uppers with bold black
marks set against orange background, with white marks near tip,
underside mottled gray-brown with silver 'J' mark on underside
of hindwing.
Habitat   Clearings, waysides, streamsides.
Flight period   One, July as hibernator.
Distribution   British Columbia to Nova Scotia, south to
Colorado and Georgia.

♂♀♂

Western/California Tortoiseshell

Nymphalis californica

Identification   Uppers with broad dark margins and black spots on leading edge of forewing, hindwing mostly rich orange, unspotted in center, underside mostly very dark with row of blue spots near margin.
Habitat   Waysides, foothills, canyons.
Flight period   May as hibernator.
Distribution   British Columbia to North Carolina, south to California and Georgia.

♂♀♂

Fire-rim/Milbert's Tortoiseshell *Aglais milberti*

Identification   Bright orange bands cross uppers, dark toward base, inside of dark margin punctuated with blue spots on hindwing, underside dark to inside, variable as subspecies.
Habitat   Waysides, meadows, streams, urban.
Flight period   Three, May–August.
Distribution   Alaska to Newfoundland, southwest to California and New Mexico.

Mourning Cloak
Nymphalis antiopa

Identification   Strong cream-yellow border and row of blue spots toward margin of rich maroon uppers, underside dark, variable as subspecies.
Habitat   Numerous types from forest edge to urban.
Flight period   Continuous.
Distribution   Most of United States and Canada, except most of arctic region.

American Painted Lady *Cynthia virginiensis*

Identification   Key feature is pair of two large eye-spots toward margins of underside of hindwings.
Habitat   Flowery waysides, streamsides, canyons.
Flight period   Three, March- October.
Distribution   Most of United States, reaching southward and northward.

♂♀♂

Painted Lady *Cynthia cardui*

Identification Underside of hindwing has four unequal
eye-spots toward margin, variable as subspecies.
Habitat Flowery areas in many habitat types.
Flight period Continuous in south.
Distribution Most of United States, northward into Canada
to within Arctic Circle.

West Coast Lady/ Western Painted Lady

Vanessa carye

♂♀

Identification Spots on
underside hindwing are
indistinct, forewing is slightly
indented and no white bar on
forewing toward its base.
Habitat Flowery areas in
many habitat types.
Flight period Continuous
in south.
Distribution British
Columbia to Mexico.

♂♀♂

Red Admiral *Vanessa atalanta*

Identification   Red-orange band crosses black forewing,
which has white marks toward tip, red-orange margin on
hindwing, underside with unique mottled pattern.
Habitat   All types of habitat.
Flight period   Continuous in south.
Distribution   Most of United States, southward, and
northward to Hudson Bay and Alaska.

Buckeye

Precis coenia

Identification   Four
eye-spots on forewing
(two large, two small)
are distinctive, with white
band enclosing larger
eye-spots.
Habitat   Waysides and
meadows.
Flight period
Continuous in south.

♂♀

Distribution   Southern
United States, venturing
northward into southeast
Canada.

White Peacock

Anartia jatrophae

Identification Female larger, light gray-brown, wings crossed by dark veins, two small spots on forewing, one on hindwing.
Habitat Swamps, watersides.
Flight period Continuous.
Distribution Florida, Texas, northward.

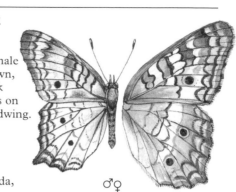

♂♀

♂♀

White Admiral *Limenitis arthemis*

Identification Bluish marginal spots around uppers and distinctive white band crosses uppers, underside shows white band against brown and red-brick background, variable as subspecies, some with blue uppers.
Habitat Woodlands and glades.
Flight period Two, June–August.
Distribution Alaska to Florida, Arizona and New Mexico.

Viceroy
Limenitis archippus ♂♀

Identification Thin black line crosses veins of upper hindwing, otherwise rich brown background color, with black veins and white spots in dark marginal band, variable as subspecies.
Habitat Waysides, streamsides, meadows.
Flight period Three, May–September.
Distribution North West Territories to Newfoundland, south to Florida, patchily in southwest United States, south into Mexico.

Western/ Weidemeyer's Admiral
Limenitis weidemeyer ♂♀

Identification Undersides with much white, especially hindwing, which has bluey-white near base and bold band crossing wing, uppers black with white band.
Habitat Waysides, streams, urban.
Flight period One, May–August.
Distribution Western United States but not coastal.

Orange Tip/Lorquin's Admiral

Limenitis lorquini

Identification   As name suggests, it has buff or orange tips to forewings, as well as off-white bands across black wings. Underside has white bands over a russet background.
Habitat   Waysides, streamsides, margins of lakes.
Flight period   Two, April–September.
Distribution   British Columbia to Baja California.

Red Rim *Biblis hyperia*

Identification   Distinctive red band on black hindwing, repeated on underside, but with brown background color.
Habitat   Woods.   **Flight period**   Several.
Distribution   Texas, and southward.

Sister/ California Sister

Limenitis bredowii

Identification Key features are broken white band on forewing with bright orange blobs near tip, underside with blue, cream and orange bands, variable as subspecies.
Habitat Oakwoods and foothills.
Flight period Two, April–October.
Distribution Washington state to Mexico.

Goatweed Butterfly

Anaea andria

Identification
Male has bright orange uppers, female is more subdued with lots of brown mottling and darker area toward margins of its uppers, undersides are fairly similar.
Habitat Waysides, woodlands, and fields.
Flight period April–October.
Distribution Arizona to Kentucky and Florida.

Hackberry Emperor/Hackberry Butterfly

Asterocampa celtis

Identification
Forewings black with
white marks, rows of
spots on inside of margin
cross hindwing, undersides
gray-blue, variable as
subspecies.
Habitat   Waysides,
woods, urban.
Flight period   Three,
March–October.
Distribution   From
Minnesota to Arizona and Florida.

♂♀

♂♀♀

Tawny Emperor *Asterocampa clyton*

Identification   Forewing lighter than hindwing and not
distinct spots, hindwing with row of black spots, patterned
forewing has yellowish and black marks, variable as subspecies.
Habitat   Waysides and woods.
Flight period   Continuous in south.
Distribution   New Mexico to Maine and Florida.

Empress Flora

Asterocampa flora   ♂♀

Identification   Strong black marks distributed evenly over
uppers, and forewing only slightly lighter centrally.
Habitat   Woods and coastal scrub.
Flight period   Two, March–September.
Distribution   Georgia, Florida.

♂♀

Mimic

♂   *Hypolimnas misippus*

Identification   Sexes completely different, male with purple-
edged white spots on uppers, female bright orange with white
spots toward forewing tips, underside large white blotches set
against tan-to-reddish background color.
Habitat   Waysides and woods.
Flight period   Continuous.   **Distribution**   Florida.

Browns

Southern Pearly Eye/Pearly Eye

Lethe portlandia

♂♀

Identification   Forewing eye-spots not aligned in straight line, underside eye-spots pronounced, spots very variable and, when pupilled, only on underside, variable as subspecies.
Habitat   Woods, streams, gardens.
Flight period Continuous, April–November.
Distribution   Southeast United States, except most of Florida.

Northern Pearly Eye

Lethe anthedon

Identification Forewing eye-spots nearly in straight line, spots on underside not so pronounced, fewer dark markings than Southern Pearly Eye.
Habitat   Waysides and clearings.
Flight period   Two, June–September.
Distribution   Alberta to Nova Scotia, south to Louisiana.

♂♀

♀ ## Creole Pearly Eye
Lethe creola

Identification   Distinctive curved leading edge to forewing, male with sex brands highlighted along veins, row of eye-spots on uppers repeated below.
Habitat   Waysides, especially streamsides with bamboo.
Flight period   Continuous, June–September.
Distribution   Southeast United States, except most of Florida.

Marsh-eyed Brown/ Eyed Brown
Lethe eurydice

Identification   Underside velvety-brown with two washmarks, and row of ringed and pupilled spots running inside of margins, variable as subspecies.
Habitat   Damp fields and meadows with sedges.
Flight period   Two, June–August.
Distribution   North West Territories to Quebec, and south to central United States.

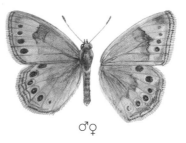

Woods Eye Brown/ Appalachian Brown

Lethe appalachia

♂♀

Identification Underside with three 'hairstreak-like' lines, one of which is straight, series of eye-spots runs around underside of wings both sides.
Habitat Waysides and woodlands.
Flight period Two, June–October.
Distribution Most of eastern half of United States.

♂♂

Little Wood Satyr *Megisto cymela*

Identification Two black eye-spots on forewing are repeated on underside, as well as on underside hindwing, two distinct lines cross undersides, variable as forms.
Habitat Grassy, woody areas.
Flight period One, May–September.
Distribution Eastern half of United States and into southeastern Canada.

$\sigma^7 \varphi \sigma^7$

Ringlet *Coenonympha tullia*

Identification   Often rich orange to underside of forewing, with gray underside of hindwing, some subspecies dark gray or very light below, very variable as subspecies.
Habitat   Grassy areas.
Flight period   Continuous, May–September.
Distribution   Alaska to California to Newfoundland.

$\sigma^7 \varphi \varphi$

Red Satyr *Megisto rubricata*

Identification   Named after rosy flush on underside of forewing, this insect has a single spot on its forewing and two set in a band on underside hindwing, variable as subspecies.
Habitat   Grassy areas, woodlands.
Flight period   Continuous, February–December.
Distribution   Arizona to Kansas, southward.

♂♀♀

Pine Satyr *Paramacera allyni*

Identification   Forewing eye-spot prominent, rows of eye-spots around inside of margin of underside hindwing, with two wavy lines crossing hindwing.
Habitat   Pine forests.   **Flight period**   Two, June–September.
Distribution   Arizona to Texas, southward.

♂♀

Wood/Large
♂ Wood Nymph
Cercyonis pegala

Identification   Two large eye-spots on forewing repeated on underside, variable-sized eye-spots occur on both upper and underside of hindwing, variable as subspecies.
Habitat   Waysides and grassy areas.
Flight period   One, June–September.
Distribution   Most of United States and southern Canada, except southwestern United States.

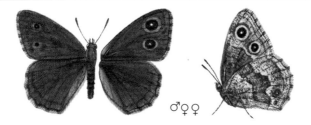

Scrub Wood/Great Basin Wood Nymph

Cercyonis sthelene

Identification   Dark uppers with two eye-spots on forewing, large in female, repeated below, underside of hindwing mottled light and dark, with or without smaller spots, variable as subspecies.
Habitat   Waysides, clearings, chaparral.
Flight period   One, June–August.
Distribution   Western United States, north into British Columbia.

Small/Dark Wood Nymph *Cercyonis oetus*

Identification   Eye-spots on female forewing slightly larger than those of male, underside dark to light with zig-zag line crossing underside of hindwing, variable as subspecies.
Habitat   Waysides and grassy areas.
Flight period   One, July–August.
Distribution   Western United States and into southwestern Canada, but not coastal.

Two-dot Rossi

Erebia rossii

♂♀

Identification Named after two pupils or spots enclosed or close together on forewing, otherwise dark wings, slightly lighter in female, with orangey tinges toward base of underside forewing, variable as subspecies.
Habitat Alpine meadows.
Flight period One, June–July.
Distribution Alaska to Baffin Island.

♂♀♀

White-spot/Spruce Bog Alpine *Erebia disa*

Identification Uppers brown-black, often with four eye-spots on forewing, lighter in female, underside rich brown-black with repeated eye-spots, variable as subspecies.
Habitat Bogs, taiga. **Flight period** One, June-July.
Distribution Alaska to Newfoundland.

Common Alpine

Erebia epipsodea

♂♀

Identification Dark wings, with twin spots on forewing and other spots both on forewing and hindwing, all set in a band of pale red-orange, undersides dark chocolate background color.
Habitat Grassy areas, including meadows.
Flight period One, June–August.
Distribution Alaska to Manitoba, and south to New Mexico.

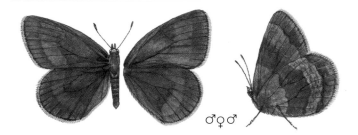

♂♀♂

White-band/Banded Alpine *Erebia fasciata*

Identification Distinctive light and dark bands cross the undersides, thus its name, male uppers slightly darker than female, absence of spots.
Habitat Bogs, tundra. **Flight period** One, June–July.
Distribution Alaska to Hudson Bay.

♂♀♂

Red-disk/Red-disked Alpine *Erebia discoidalis*

Identification Named after red flush on forewing, otherwise overall color somber, lack of eye-spots on forewing, and pattern repeated on underside.
Habitat Meadows and bogs.
Flight period One, May–July.
Distribution Alaska to Quebec.

Grasshopper/Riding's Satyr *Neominois ridingsii*

Identification Unique color and patterns, reminiscent of striations in grasshoppers, two forewing eye-spots with pupils.
Habitat Grassy areas, prairies, meadows.
Flight period Two, June–August.
Distribution Alberta and Saskatchewan, south to Arizona and New Mexico.

Brown/Chryxus Arctic *Oeneis chryxus*

Identification
Uppers and underside very pale to light brown, with small eye-spots on all wings, variable as subspecies.
Habitat Grassy areas, tundra.
Flight period One, May–August.
Distribution Alaska to Newfoundland, south to New Mexico and California.

Rocky Mountain/ Uhler's Arctic

Oeneis uhleri

Identification Honey-colored uppers and paler underside of forewing, underside of hindwing strongly waved and mottled, number of eye-spots variable, variable as subspecies.
Habitat Clearings, meadows, prairie, taiga.
Flight period Two, May–August.
Distribution Alaska to New Mexico, disjointedly.

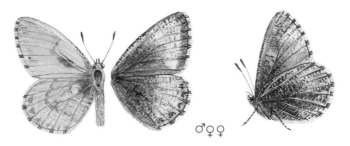

♂♀♀

Arctic Grayling *Oeneis bore*

Identification Very pale wings with wave lines crossing underside of hindwing, spots almost absent, variable as subspecies.
Habitat Tundra, hammocks.
Flight period One, June–July.
Distribution Alaska south erratically to Wyoming, Newfoundland.

♂♀♂

Forest/Jutta Arctic *Oeneis jutta*

Identification Dark gray and somber background color, highlighted by pale orange band or series of marks enclosing black spots crossing uppers, underside of hindwing mottled, variable as subspecies.
Habitat Bogs, clearings, taiga.
Flight period One, May–August.
Distribution Alaska to Newfoundland, south erratically to Wyoming.

$\male\female\female$

Mottled/Melissa Arctic *Oeneis melissa*

Identification   A dirty tan-colored butterfly with dark base to underside of hindwing, variable as subspecies.
Habitat   Grassy areas, tundra.
Flight period   One, June–August.
Distribution   Alaska to New Mexico somewhat erratically, and to Newfoundland.

Banded/ Polixenes Arctic

Oeneis polixenes

$\male\female$

Identification   Named after broad dark band which crosses underside of hindwing, otherwise wings somber-colored and unmarked, variable as subspecies.
Habitat   Grassy areas, tundra.
Flight period One, June–August.
Distribution   Alaska to Newfoundland, parcels of distribution to New Mexico.

Milkweeds

♂♀

♂

Monarch *Danaus plexippus*

Identification   Large butterfly with rich orange-red ground color, black veins, and black border with white spots around wings.
Habitat   Flowery waysides, valleys, gardens.
Flight period   Several.
Distribution   All of United States, northward to Hudson Bay, and southward into Mexico.

♂♀

♂

Queen *Danaus gilippus*

Identification Brown-orange ground color, black veins and black border with white spots around border, variable as subspecies.

Habitat Woodlands, fields, meadows, desert.

Flight period Continuous in south.

Distribution East to west United States as far north as Great Lakes.

Snouts

♂♀ ♀

Snout/Southern Snout Butterfly

Libytheana carinenta

Identification   Characteristic indented forewing shape,
angular hindwing, and 'snout' features of mouthparts, dark
brown wings with white and orange marks, variable as
subspecies.
Habitat   Woodland clearings and edges.
Flight period   Continuous in south.
Distribution   All southern states of United States, northward
to Great Lakes.

Snout Butterfly

Libytheana bachmanii

♂♀

Identification   Large white
spots and orange patches on
brown forewings, conspicuous
orange patch on hindwing,
underside hindwing gray with
dark line from base, forewing
orange toward base.
Habitat   Woods and clearings.
Flight period   Continuous
in south.
Distribution   Southwestern
United States and Mexico,
north to Great Lakes and New
England.

METALMARKS
HAIRSTREAKS
HARVESTER
COPPERS, BLUES

*B*utterflies of this group are small and colorful, they like wild flowers, and are often found in towns and cities. The hairstreaks are the most numerous and many of them have a tiny 'hairstreak line' running across the undersides of the wings. Blues and coppers are named after their colors, and males usually have more flashy colors than females.

Some members of the blues are associated with ants in their caterpillar stage.

Metalmarks

Mormon Metalmark
Apodemia mormo

♂♀

Identification Attractively colored with white spots on uppers against dark brown hindwing and chestnut base of forewing, underside has repeat pattern of uppers on more subdued background color, variable as subspecies.
Habitat Wide range from coast to mountains.
Flight period One–two, March–October.
Distribution Entire west coast of United States to Montana.

Nais Metalmark/Coppermark *Apodemia nais*

Identification Distinctive bright copper color of underside forewing gave rise to this species being thought of as a copper. Underside of hindwing white with black spots like checkerspots, variable as subspecies.
Habitat Chaparral, foothills, canyons.
Flight period One, June–October.
Distribution Arizona to Colorado and New Mexico.

♂♀

Gray/Mesquite Metalmark *Apodemia palmerii*

♂♀

Identification Uppers dark brown, checkered with prominent white spots, underside very pale tan with repeat pattern of upperside.
Habitat Deserts with mesquite.
Flight period Three, April–November.
Distribution Southern California to west Texas.

Northern Metalmark *Calephelis borealis*

Identification   Rich brown-chestnut uppers crossed by fine tracery and rows of dots, underside rich tan peppered with tiny black dots which fall roughly into rows.
Habitat   Clearings on limestone.
Flight period   One, June–July.
Distribution   Kentucky, Virginia, Pennsylvania.

Swamp Metalmark *Calephelis muticum*

Identification   Brown background with black spots on uppers, delightful rich orange underside with spots and dashes.
Habitat   Swamps, bogs, damp meadows.
Flight period   One–two, July–September.
Distribution   South and east of Great Lakes to Arkansas.

Little Metalmark *Calephelis virginiensis*

Identification   Russet uppers of male with black markings in close rows of dots and lines, underside tan covered with tiny dots.
Habitat   Grassy areas and clearings.
Flight period   Three, April–October, continuous in Florida.
Distribution   Louisiana to North Carolina southward.

Hairstreaks

Colorado Hairstreak *Hypaurotis crysalus*

Identification   Violet sheen over most of forewings and orange marginal marks, underside with 'W' mark, and orange and blue near tail, variable as subspecies.
Habitat   Gambel oak woods.
Flight period   One, June–September, depending on altitude.
Distribution   Utah south to New Mexico.

Live-oak Hairstreak *Habrodais grunus*

Identification   Rounded wings, burnt-orange uppers, light brown undersides with thin hairstreak line, variable as subspecies.
Habitat   Oak woodland.
Flight period   One, June–August.
Distribution   Washington state to Baja California.

Atala/Coontie Hairstreak *Eumaeus atala*

Identification Orange abdomen, blue-green luster on
forewing and underside of hindwing with sparkling green dots.
Habitat Woodland edges and hammocks.
Flight period Continuous.
Distribution Tip of Florida only.

White-rim Cycad/Cycad Hairstreak

Eumaeus minijas

Identification Blue
dusting on forewing
of male on dark
background, female
with green dusting over
black background.
Habitat Clearings
with cycads.
Flight period All
year as immigrant from
Mexico.
Distribution Texas,
Florida.

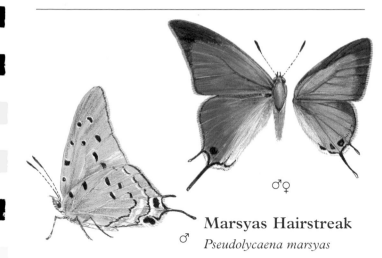

♂♀

Marsyas Hairstreak

♂ *Pseudolycaena marsyas*

Identification   Stunning 'Morpho-like' blue on male uppers, iridescent green-blue on female, and two tails.
Habitat   Waysides and scrub.
Flight period   August–September.
Distribution   Stray into Texas.

♂♀ ♀

Double-spotted Slate/Zebrina Hairstreak

Thereus zebrina

Identification   Shiny blue uppers on male, white-brown on female.
Habitat   Dry forest and scrub.
Flight period   September–November.
Distribution   Stray into Texas.

Great Purple/Blue Hairstreak *Atlides halesus*

Identification Male iridescent blue with green base of forewings, female blue at base of two tails.
Habitat Variety of habitats with mistletoe-bound trees.
Flight period Two, February–April, July–October.
Distribution Southeastern and southwestern United States.

♂♀

White-M Hairstreak

Parrhasius m-album

♂

♂♀

Identification Iridescent blue on forewings of both sexes, with thick dark marginal band, orange, black, and blue spots near 'M' mark at base of two tails.
Habitat Grassy meadows and clearings.
Flight period Three in south, two in north; February–August.
Distribution New York to Texas, including southern states, except Florida.

Large Brilliant/ Aquamarine Hairstreak

Oenomaus

ortygnus

♂♀

♂

Identification Iridescent blue with touch of green at base, gray with bold black marks, and aquamarine near base of two tails.
Habitat Scrub. **Flight period** December.
Distribution Stray into Texas.

Nightshade/Jade-blue Hairstreak

Arawacus jada

Identification Dark brown tips to forewings, blue-purple uppers, white with watermarks below, single tail.
Habitat Forest edges and clearings.
Flight period Continuous.
Distribution Rare stray into Arizona.

♂♀

♂♀♀

Brown Elfin *Callophrys augustus*

Identification Dark brown above with pronounced male cell, light brown below, variable as subspecies.
Habitat Various, including glades, chaparral, deserts.
Flight period One, February–June, depending on elevation; earlier and later in western United States.
Distribution Widespread, Alaska to Newfoundland, south to Georgia and Baja California.

♂♀♂

Desert/Early Elfin *Callophrys fotis*

Identification Gray-brown above, darker in female with white-gray edge to underside of forewing, wide silver-gray bar crossing underside of hindwing.
Habitat Western desert.　**Flight period** One, March–May.
Distribution California, Utah, Arizona, Colorado, New Mexico.

Stonecrop Elfin/Moss Elfin *Callophrys mossii*

Identification   Male with dark uppers and banded margin, female dark orange-brown uppers, reddish edge to wings below and whitish hairstreak line, forms and subspecies.
Habitat   Canyons, ravines, hillsides.
Flight period   One, February–June.
Distribution   Oregon, Utah to California.

Hoary Elfin *Callophrys polios*

Identification   Dark brown above, with faintly banded white and black edging above and below.
Habitat   Rocky sites, scrub and heathland.
Flight period   One, March–June.
Distribution   Alaska to Baja California and to Newfoundland and south to Georgia and Alabama.

Frosted Elfin *Callophrys irus*

Identification   Male with dark brown above, female orangey with dark brown at base, lighter brown on underside, with spot toward base of stubby tail.
Habitat   Waysides and scrubby areas.
Flight period   One, April–May.
Distribution   New York to Georgia, and Texas.

Woodland/ Henry's Elfin

Callophrys henrici

σ♀

Identification   Male lacks forewing stigma on very dark brown wings, female lighter brown, variable as subspecies.
Habitat   Clearings, woodland edges, scrub.
Flight period   One, March–April.
Distribution   Eastern half of United States.

σ♀♀

Spruce-Bog/Bog Elfin *Callophrys lanoraieensis*

Identification   Dark brown above with checkered edge in both sexes, mottled underside zig-zags on underside hindwing.
Habitat   Spruce bogs.   **Flight period**   One, May–June.
Distribution   Southeastern Canada and northeastern United States.

σ♀σ

Eastern Pine Elfin *Callophrys niphon*

Identification   Male brown above with checkered edge, female with orange blotches on wings, black hairstreak mark crossing underside of wings, including black zig-zag marks.
Habitat   Pine and spruce woods.
Flight period   One, March–June.
Distribution   Eastern States, except Florida, and from Great Lakes to Alberta.

Western Pine Elfin

Callophrys eryphon

Identification Male darker brown uppers than female, checkered margins, underside with zig-zags and checkered margins.
Habitat Spruce bogs, pine forests, and canyons.
Flight period One, May–June.
Distribution Southwestern states, north and east to Maine.

♂♀

♂♀♀ ♀

Beargrass/Sandia Hairstreak

Callophrys mcfarlandii

Identification Male olive-brown uppers, female soft brown, underside hindwing lemon-green with white hairstreak line.
Habitat Beargrass-dominated habitats.
Flight period Multiple, February–July.
Distribution New Mexico, Texas to Mexico.

Succulent/ Xami Hairstreak

Callophrys xami

Identification Dark gray above, darker in females, light brown undersides, hairstreak line crossing both wings, two tails with dark tips.
Habitat Rocky sites.
Flight period Multiple, April–December, variable.
Distribution Mexico, Texas, and Arizona.

♂♀

Blue Mistletoe/ Thicket Hairstreak

Callophrys spinetorum

Identification   Blue-gray uppers, reddish-brown undersides and white hairstreak mark with 'W' mark by two tails.
Habitat   Conifer woodlands.
Flight period   One at east of range (June–July), two in west (March–September).
Distribution   British Columbia to Mexico, east to Colorado.

Brown Mistletoe/ Johnson's Hairstreak

Callophrys johnsoni

Identification   Slate-green uppers in both sexes, with two tails, one small, one large, red-brown underside.
Habitat   Conifer forests.   **Flight period**   One, June–July.
Distribution   British Columbia to California, Oregon.

Nelson's Hairstreak

Callophrys nelsoni

Identification   Male with brown wings with three orange lunules near tail, and orange suffusion over forewing, female with orange suffusion over all wings with dark margins.
Habitat   Conifer forests.
Flight period   One, May–July.
Distribution   British Columbia to Baja California, Nevada.

♂♀♀

Juniper Hairstreak *Callophrys siva*

Identification   Gray-brown uppers with orange suffusion over uppers, bright green below crossed by white hairstreak mark, and two pairs of unequal tails.
Habitat   Scrubby areas, canyons and scarps.
Flight period   One–three, June–September.
Distribution   Washington state to California, east to Texas.

Loki/Skinner's
Hairstreak *Callophrys loki*

♂♀

Identification   Male with dark gray-brown uppers, orange suffusion over uppers of female, green below.
Habitat   Juniper woodland.
Flight period   Two–three, March–October.
Distribution   British Columbia to Baja California.

♂♀♀

Cedar/Olive Hairstreak *Callophrys gryneus*

Identification   Brown uppers with dark margins, sex brand in male, olive-green underside of male hindwing, turquoise band at margin and two unequal tails, highly variable as subspecies.
Habitat   Hills and fields with red cedar.
Flight period   Two, April–May, July–August.
Distribution   Mostly eastern United States.

White Cedar/Hessel's Hairstreak

Callophrys hesseli

Identification   Dark brown to reddish on uppers, green speckled undersides with white irregular hairstreak line of crescents on underside hindwing, two unequal pairs of tails, sex brand in male.
Habitat   Swamps and bogs.
Flight period   Two, May–July.
Distribution   Eastern seaboard states.

♂♀

♂♀♂

Bramble Green/Coastal Green Hairstreak

Callophrys dumetorum

Identification   Uppers gray-brown in both sexes, small sex brand evident on male forewings, underside bluish-green crossed by whitish dashes, no tails.
Habitat   Chaparral, canyons, wastelands.
Flight period   One, April–May.
Distribution   Mid-California coast, southward.

♂♀♀

Green/Immaculate Green Hairstreak

Callophrys affinis

Identification   Dark brown on uppers of each sex, broken white hairstreak line, no tails.
Habitat   Sagelands.   **Flight period**   One, April–June.
Distribution   British Columbia to Colorado.

Canyon/
Green Hairstreak

Callophrys affinis apama ♂♀♂

Identification   Gray-brown above, light green below, with white spots as hairstreak line, subspecies of *C. affinis*, also regarded as having true species status.
Habitat   Mountains up to 10,000 feet.
Flight period   Uncertain, March–August.
Distribution   Wyoming, Utah, Arizona, New Mexico, Colorado, Mexico.

♂♀♀

Little Green/White-lined Green Hairstreak

Callophrys sheridanii

Identification   Dark brown above in both sexes, continuous white hairstreak line crossing undersides of green wings, no tail.
Habitat   Mountains to 10,000 feet.
Flight period   One, April–May.
Distribution   British Columbia to New Mexico.

♂♀♀

Orange/Behr's Hairstreak *Satyrium behrii*

Identification   Orange uppers with black background and margin in both sexes, gray below with rows of speckles, no tail.
Habitat   Scrub, foothills, deserts.
Flight period   One, June–July.
Distribution   British Columbia to New Mexico and California.

Sooty Hairstreak *Satyrium fuliginosum*

Identification   Rich dark brown over all uppers, sooty underside
with hairstreak line as series of black dots crossing wings.
Habitat   Sagebrush and lupin meadows in mountains.
Flight period   One, May–August.
Distribution   British Columbia to Colorado and California.

Northern Willow/Acadian Hairstreak

Satyrium acadica

Identification   Dark brown
uppers with single orange spot
near tail, male with large sex
brands, silver gray below with
blue spot near tail.
Habitat   Willow sites of
streams and meadows.
Flight period   One, June–July.
Distribution   Across United
States and Canada in broad band
from Washington state to Maine.

Western/
California
Hairstreak

Satyrium californica

Identification   Dark brown uppers of male with orange
lunules near tail, orange suffusion on uppers of female,
hairstreak bands of black and white and marginal orange lunules
on undersides of hindwings.
Habitat Foothills, chaparral. **Flight period** One, May–August.
Distribution   British Columbia to Colorado and California.

Western Willow/Sylvan Hairstreak

Satyrium sylvinus

Identification   Male light brown above, female darker, gray to white-gray below and very sparse on spots, especially near margin, tail to tailless, variable as subspecies.
Habitat   Foothills and mountains.
Flight period   Onc, May–August.
Distribution   British Columbia to Baja California, and east to New Mexico.

Scrub Oak/ Edward's Hairstreak

Satyrium edwardsii

Identification   Dark brown uppers, mellow brown below with blue spot near tiny tail, streak of black spots crosses undersides of hindwing.
Habitat   Scrub oaks.   **Flight period**   One, June–July.
Distribution   Eastern United States, though not throughout the southern states.

Banded Hairstreak

Satyrium calanus

Identification   Rich dark brown above, male with pronounced sex brand, blue spot near tail large in male, two rows of hairstreak lines cross undersides, more pronounced in male.
Habitat   Waysides, urban areas, deciduous forest edges.
Flight period   One, June–July.
Distribution   Eastern half of United States, except tip of Florida, isolated population centered on Kansas, and across southern Canada.

Hickory Hairstreak

Satyrium caryaevorus

Identification   Brown-black above in both sexes, sex brand obvious on male forewing, underside silvery-gray, blue spot near unequal pair of tails but lacking large orange spots or bands of similar species.
Habitat   Deciduous woodlands, waysides.
Flight period   One, June–July.
Distribution   Quebec, Minnesota, and states to Iowa, Kentucky.

Sweetleaf/King's Hairstreak *Satyrium kingi*

Identification   Blue spot on underside of hindwing has lunule of orange behind it, and other orange marks inside two unequal-sized tails.
Habitat   Swamps, hammocks, coastal deciduous woods.
Flight period   One, May–August, variable.
Distribution   Virginia to Mississippi coast.

Striped Hairstreak

Satyrium liparops

Identification   Rich dark brown above in both sexes, three broken hairstreak lines below, with orange and blue near two tails of male.
Habitat   Deciduous woodlands, scrub, hedgerows.
Flight period   One, July–August.
Distribution   Three-fourths of United States, across southern Canada from British Columbia to Quebec.

Gold Hunter's Hairstreak *Satyrium auretorum*

Identification   A drab butterfly with dark brown above, caramel below with faint hairstreak line, dull blue spot near short tail.
Habitat   Oak woods and scrub.   **Flight period**   One, May–July.
Distribution   California to Baja California.

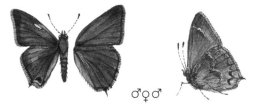

Chaparral/Mountain Mahogany Hairstreak

Satyrium tetra

Identification   Dark brown uppers, lighter in female, sex brand on male forewing, underside dark brown with dark-gray base to hindwing and tiny blue spot near tail, tail very short in male.
Habitat   Chaparral.   **Flight period**   One, June–July.
Distribution   Oregon to Mexico.

Buckthorn/ Hedgerow Hairstreak

Satyrium saepium

Identification   Orange-brown uppers with dark margins, dark brown below, white hairstreak across wings, blue spot near tail.
Habitat   Great variety from chaparral, conifer forests and roadsides.
Flight period   One, May–September, variable with altitude.
Distribution   British Columbia to Baja California east to Colorado.

Southern Oak/Southern Hairstreak

Fixsenia favonius

Identification   Dark brown wings in both sexes with light margins, orange marks on or absent from upper forewing and hindwing, blue and orange spot near two tails, variable as subspecies.
Habitat   Oak woods, hammocks.
Flight period   One, May–June.
Distribution   Virginia to Texas southward.

Northern Hairstreak

Fixsenia favonius ontario

Identification   Large blue spot on underside of hindwing, accompanied by large orange spot, subspecies of *favonius*.
Habitat   Oak woodlands and scrub.
Flight period   One, April–June, variable to latitude.
Distribution   Ontario, Massachussetts to Texas.

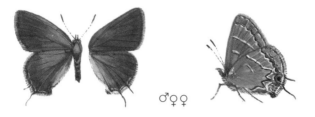

Soapberry Hairstreak *Phaeostrymon alcestis*

Identification   Uppers mellow brown, undersides smooth brown with white hairstreak line ending in 'VW' near two tails.
Habitat   Canyons and roadsides with soapberry.
Flight period   One, April–July.
Distribution   Kansas to Arizona in three distinct populations.

Verde Azul/ Amethyst Hairstreak

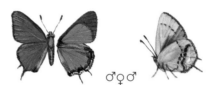

Chlorostrymon maesites

Identification   Iridescent amethyst-blue in male, female with dark tip to forewing, below mustard-orange.
Habitat   Hammocks.
Flight period   All year in Florida, June in Texas.
Distribution   Stray from Mexico.

Silver-banded Hairstreak *Chlorostrymon simaethis*

Identification   Male uppers with amethyst sheen, female with dark tips to forewings and iridescent blue at bases of wings, green underside with hairstreak line.
Habitat   Arid scrub.   **Flight period**   Two, April–December.
Distribution   California, Arizona, Texas, Mexico.

Turquoise/Early Hairstreak *Erora laeta*

Identification   Dark forewings with blue sheen toward base, stronger in female, undersides with distinctive caramel color and hairstreak lines across light brown-silver background.
Habitat   Beechwoods and forests.
Flight period   One, March–August variable.
Distribution   Eastern Canada to New England, south to South Carolina.

Red-banded Hairstreak *Calycopis cecrops*

Identification   Male dark brown above, female suffused with blue, caramel below with red-orange hairstreak line, blue spot near two tails.
Habitat   Waysides, woodland edges.
Flight period   Three, April–October.
Distribution   Southeastern states only.

Leda Hairstreak

Ministrymon leda

Identification   Male silver-blue dusting toward base of gray forewings, female turquoise-blue underside with orange hairstreak line across pale brown background, two unequal tails.
Habitat   Scrub, foothills, and forests.
Flight period   Two, May–November.
Distribution   California, Arizona, New Mexico, Mexico.

♂♀♂

Grizzled/Sonoran Hairstreak

Hypostrymon critola

Identification Distinctive black spot in center of turquoise wing of male, faint in female, which has pale silver-blue hindwing, underside streaky gray with two spots near two tails.
Habitat Desert scrub and beaches.
Flight period April–May.
Distribution Sonoran desert, Mexico, Arizona, Baja California.

♂♀♂

Gray/Common Hairstreak *Strymon melinus*

Identification Rich dark brown uppers with orange lunules between unequal tails, underside light gray with orange-white hairstreak line and orange lunules by tails.
Habitat Exploits many natural and man-made habitats.
Flight period Two–three in south, April–October.
Distribution Everywhere in United States and across southern Canada.

Catalina/ Avalon Hairstreak

Strymon avalona

♂♀♂

Identification Gray-brown uppers with orange lunules by tail, underside slate-gray with white hairstreak line.
Habitat Chaparral, waysides.
Flight period Possibly continuous, April–November.
Distribution Santa Catalina island off southern California coast.

Tarugo/Alea Hairstreak

Strymon alea

♂♀♂

Identification Uppers dark brown in both sexes, black marks to inside of whitish margins, underside grayish with white lunules round edge of wings, shades of orange on hindwing and blue spots near tail.
Habitat Desert and semi-arid areas.
Flight period Continuous, February–December.
Distribution Mexico to Texas.

White-stripe/Yoyoa Hairstreak *Strymon yojoa*

♂♀

Identification Dark brown uppers with black marginal spots highlighted by white edging, underside mottled gray-orange hairstreak line, two spots near tail.
Habitat Coniferous forests, clearings, scrub.
Flight period Continuous.
Distribution Stray into Texas.

Dotted/Columella Hairstreak

Strymon columella

Identification   Dark brown uppers with black marginal spots in both sexes, undersides with hairstreak as spots, marginal spots and orange, blue, and black spots by tail.
Habitat   Desert and subtropical areas.
Flight period   Continuous in Texas, two in southern California.
Distribution   Southwestern and southeastern United States.

Red-crescent/ Reddish Hairstreak *Strymon rufofusca*

Identification   Both sexes with rich brown uppers, thin tails with black spots, and orange lunules around base.
Habitat   Clearings in coniferous forest, waysides.
Flight period   Continuous, March–December.
Distribution   Texas.

Spotted/Cestri Hairstreak *Strymon cestri*

Identification   Both sexes with dark uppers and irregular feathering on margin of wings, female with purple sheen on half of hindwing, underside with unique wavy pattern.
Habitat   Watercourses, riverside scrub.
Flight period   Continuous.   **Distribution**   Texas.

Coral Hairstreak *Harkenclenus titus*

Identification   Very dark brown over pointed wings of male, male sex scales prominent, female larger with rounded wingtips, underside caramel with ring of orange lunules.
Habitat   Meadows, clearings, canyons.
Flight period   One, June–August.
Distribution   Across United States and Canada, except Pacific coast, along Gulf coast and Florida.

Harvester

Harvester *Feniseca tarquinius*

Identification   Orange with black/brown forewings, forewing margin bulges out slightly, underside hindwing with small circular marks toward base.
Habitat   Damp woods.
Flight period   Two in north, continuous in south, February–December.
Distribution   Eastern half of North America, north to Great Lakes.

Coppers

♂♀♂

Small Copper/American/Flame Copper

Lycaena phlaeas

Identification   Uppers coppery interspersed with dark spots and dark band to forewings, hindwing with copper at edges.
Habitat   Flowery meadows, waste ground.
Flight period   One to several, April–October in south.
Distribution   Widely distributed and well within the Arctic Circle.

Lustrous Copper

Lycaena cupreus

♂♀

Identification   The smallest American copper, male brighter copper than female, thick dark margin to undersides of hindwing, variable as subspecies.
Habitat   Alpine meadows.
Flight period   June–August.
Distribution   Western United States, and southwestern Canada.

Bronze Copper

Lycaena hyllus

Identification Largest of the typical coppers, male with purple sheen and orange band on margin of upper hindwing, white underside of hindwing.
Habitat Docks and knotweed habitats such as meadows and ditches.
Flight period Two, June–July and August–October.
Distribution North West Territories to Maine and south to Wyoming and Arkansas.

♂♀

♂♀♂

Forest/Mariposa Copper *Lycaena mariposa*

Identification Male with purple tinge and darker border, underside hindwing gray, forewing underside light copper.
Habitat Bogs and wet meadows.
Flight period One, July–August.
Distribution Yukon to Wyoming and California.

Nivalis/Lilac-bordered/Lilac-edged Copper

Lycaena nivalis

Identification Dark upper forewing of male with faint purple sheen and orange lunules on hindwing, female with dark orange spots on forewing, variable as subspecies.
Habitat Mountain meadows and clearings.
Flight period One, July–August.
Distribution Yukon to Colorado and California.

♂♀

Purplish Copper ♂♀♂
Lycaena helloides

Identification Male gray uppers with purple sheen to dark edge on forewing and hindwing, orange lunules around edge of hindwing, female with dark orange spots around margins, rest of wing suffused in copper with black spots; subspecies.
Habitat Meadows and waysides from sea-level to mountains.
Flight period Many, year-round in southern California, May–September elsewhere.
Distribution Wide-ranging from Arctic Circle to Baja California, and east to Great Lakes.

Cinquefoil/ Dorcas Copper
Lycaena dorcas

♂♀

Identification Male with strong purple sheen and broad dark margin, female brown with a few faint orange spots and black spots.
Habitat Meadows, clearings, bogs.
Flight period One, July–August.
Distribution North West Territories to Newfoundland, south to Ohio.

♂♀♂

Cranberry Bog/Bog Copper *Lycaena epixanthe*

Identification Male uppers brown with purple sheen, female charcoal with black specks, undersides very light with black specks, variable as subspecies.
Habitat Bogs and marshes. **Flight period** One, June–August.
Distribution Indiana to Newfoundland.

♂♀♂

Buckwheat/Gorgon Copper *Lycaena gorgon*

Identification Males with faint purple sheen on uppers, undersides very pale yellow with black spots and orange lunules.
Habitat Chaparral, clearings, and roadsides, always with buckwheat.
Flight period One, May–July.
Distribution Oregon to Baja California coast.

♂♀♀

Blue Copper *Lycaena heteronea*

Identification Male forewings blue, female usually brown, undersides white with black spots on forewing.
Habitat Sagelands, prairies, clearings.
Flight period One, June–August.
Distribution West to mid-west United States and southern British Columbia.

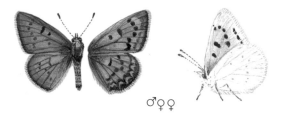

♂♀♀

Ruddy Copper *Lycaena rubidus*

Identification   Male forewing orange, lighter with darker spots in female, undersides whitish, variable as subspecies.
Habitat   Meadows and scrubby areas.
Flight period   One, June–August depending on altitude.
Distribution   Western United States and a little into Canada.

Gray/Great Gray Copper

Lycaena xanthoides

♂♀

Identification   Both sexes with gray uppers, female smaller with pronounced black spots and more orange around margin of hindwing, variable as subspecies.
Habitat   Meadows and prairies.
Flight period   One, May to July depending on subspecies.
Distribution   Central and western United States, southern Canada.

Edith's Copper

Lycaena

♂♀♂

xanthoides editha

Identification   Large underside hindwing spots, female with more orange on uppers than male, subspecies of *L. xanthoides*, also thought to have true species status.
Habitat   Meadows, clearings, roadsides.
Flight period   One, June–August.
Distribution   Northwestern United States and southwestern Alberta.

Hermes/ Yellow Copper

Lycaena hermes

♂♀♀

Identification   Sexes with quite similar dark hindwing with a little orange around base of tail, pale orange undersides with black spots on forewing.
Habitat   Chaparral.   **Flight period**   One, June–July.
Distribution   Within 100 mile radius of San Diego only.

Tailed Copper

Lycaena arota

♂♀

Identification   Male dark brown with slight purple tinge, female with copper-brown markings, both with small pointed tail which is slightly longer in the female, variable as subspecies.
Habitat   Watercourses, meadows, clearings.
Flight period   One, July–August.
Distribution   Southwestern states.

Blues

Western Pygmy Blue
Brephidium exilis

Identification Both sexes with slight purple tinge at base of brown wings, female larger than male, underside hindwing slate with black spots ringed in white, variable as subspecies.
Habitat Many semi-natural and disturbed sites with caterpillar foodplants.
Flight period Continuous, peaks in Fall.
Distribution Southwestern United States and Florida.

Tropical Striped/ Cassius Blue
Leptotes cassius

Identification Male with purple over forewing and black veins on white hindwing, female with no purple but strong black veins and dark border of forewing, pale striped watermarks over undersides.
Habitat Roadsides, grassy urban areas.
Flight period Continuous.
Distribution Florida and Georgia, and migrates northwest as far as Utah.

Striped/Marine Blue
Leptotes marina

Identification Male with turquoise over uppers, and black spot toward margin of hindwing, female with slight purple tinge at base.
Habitat Roadsides and ditches.   **Flight period** Continuous.
Distribution South Texas, migrating north to Great Lakes.

Green Hawaiian Blue/ Blackburn's Blue

♂♀♂

Vaga blackburnii

Identification   Male soft brown-purple, female bright purple with dark apex to forewing, green on underside of both sexes distinctive.
Habitat Forest clearings and edges. **Flight period** Continuous.
Distribution   Hawaii native species.

♂♀♀

Cyna Blue/Tiny Blue *Zizula cyna*

Identification   Male with violet sheen within thick black borders, female larger with pale violet within brown margins, light undersides with small round spots.
Habitat   Desert and open urban areas.
Flight period   March–September.
Distribution   South Texas, south Arizona.

♂♀♀

Caribbean/Miami Blue *Hemiargus thomasi*

Identification   Male pale blue over forewings and black spot toward hindwing margin, female with blue inside dark margins and orange lunule by two black spots on margin of upper hindwing, undersides speckled, seasonal variation, bluer in winter.
Habitat   Flowery open spaces. **Flight period** Continuous.
Distribution   Southern Florida.

Southern/ Antillean Blue

Hemiargus ceraunus ♂♀♀

Identification Male pale violet uppers, female dark apex of forewing and leading edge of hindwing, otherwise violet with two black spots on trailing edge, undersides black marks speckled against a light background, three races.
Habitat Flowery roadsides and foothills.
Flight period Continuous in Florida and Texas, March–November in California.
Distribution All southern states, but mainly Florida and California.

Mexican/Reakirt's Blue

Hemiargus isola ♂♀

Identification Male violet within dark borders of uppers, and a single black spot toward trailing edge of hindwing, female slightly larger, much darker with large spot near edge of hindwing.
Habitat Flowery man-made sites.
Flight period Continuous in south, July–October to north.
Distribution California to Mississippi, north to Saskatchewan.

Tailed Blue/ Eastern Tailed

Everes comyntas ♂♀♀

Identification Male violet-blue with row of small dots on edge of hindwing, female brown with single orange lunule, single tail, underside light with orange spot by tail.
Habitat Agricultural areas, gardens, foothills.
Flight period Three to north, Spring–Fall.
Distribution Eastern half of United States, with possible introductions to west coast.

Western Tailed Blue

Everes amyntula ♂♀♂

Identification Male with violet-blue uppers, and single tail, female violet uppers with thick dark border of forewing, orange lunules on hindwing, very pale underside with rows of pale spots on forewing.
Habitat Roadsides, clearings, meadows.
Flight period Two, Spring–Fall.
Distribution West coast states to Alaska.

Spring Sooty/ Sooty Azure

Celastrina nigra ♂♀♂

Identification Male sooty uppers, female with thick sooty margin on silvery-blue background, both sexes with light spotted underside.
Habitat Woodland meadows with foodplant.
Flight period One, April–May.
Distribution Illinois, Pennsylvania, Missouri, North Carolina.

Spring Azure

Celastrina argiolus ♂♀♂

Identification Male sky-blue uppers, female lighter blue with dark apex on forewings, undersides light blue dispersed with small spots.
Habitat Numerous habitat types from Gulf Coast to Hudson Bay. **Flight period** One to several, depending on elevation.
Distribution Extremely successful from east to west of United States into Canada to Alaska and northern Quebec.

Ladon Blue

Celastrina argiolus ladon

♂♀

Identification   Male turquoise-blue uppers, female silver-blue with dark apex and border of forewing, row of enclosed spots along margin of hindwing, subspecies of *C. argiolus*, also thought to have true species status, variable as seasonal forms.
Habitat   Wide range often near woods.
Flight period   Continuous in east.
Distribution   United States including Alaska.

Stonecrop/ Sonoran Blue

Philotes sonorensis

♂♀

Identification   Extremely attractive, male silvery-blue uppers, with pair of orange spots on forewing edge, and black tips with black spots, female same plan but orange spots merged on forewing, and orange spots on hindwing.
Habitat   Desert, canyons, chaparral.
Flight period   One, February–June.
Distribution   Southern California, Mohave desert, Colorado.

Buckwheat/ Square-spotted Blue

♂♀♂

Euphilotes battoides

Identification   Male blue uppers with row of small spots around edge of hindwing, female brown uppers with row of orange lunules on hindwing, underside warm brown, covered in black spots and orange suffusion near margin of hindwing.
Habitat   Near stands of buckwheat.
Flight period   One, coincident with foodplant flowering.
Distribution   Western United States, north to British Columbia.

Dotted Blue
Euphilotes enoptes ♂♀♀

Identification   Male violet-blue within bold brown border to uppers, wider border in hindwing, female brown uppers with faint orange band of lunules, undersides light brown covered in spots and orange lunule band.
Habitat   Desert, chaparral, sagebrush with buckwheat.
Flight period   One, coincident with foodplant flowering.
Distribution   Western United States.

Desert Buckwheat/
Rita Blue *Euphilotes rita* ♂♀♀

Identification   Male blue-violet sheen on uppers, with small dots around edges of both wings, female brown uppers with orange lunule band on hindwing, undersides fawn with black speckles and orange lunule band on hindwing.
Habitat   Deserts and grasslands.
Flight period   One, April–May.
Distribution   Southwestern United States.

♂♀♂

Colorado-plateau Blue *Euphilotes spaldingi*

Identification   Male blue uppers with faint orange band on hindwing border, female brown uppers with continuous orange band around borders of forewings and hindwings, underside with orange border and black spots over gray background.
Habitat   Prairie and scrubby areas.
Flight period   Several, May–October.
Distribution   Saskatchewan to Pennsylvania and south to Mexico and southern California.

Small Blue

Philotiella speciosa

♂♀♀

Identification　Male blue uppers, female brown uppers, both with checkered edges, underside gray with black spots, one of the smallest of butterflies.
Habitat　Desert, chaparral, washes.
Flight period　One, April–May.
Distribution　Western United States.

Arrowhead Blue

Glaucopsyche piasus

♂♀

Identification　Male blue with brown borders above, female less blue with brown borders, both with checkered margins, light arrowhead marks around margin of underside hindwings.
Habitat　Canyons and grasslands with lupine.
Flight period　One, April–July.
Distribution　Western United States into Canada.

♂♀♂

Silvery Blue　*Glaucopsyche lygdamus*

Identification　Extremely variable with 10 subspecies, male silvery-blue uppers, female dark brown with faint dusting of blue on uppers, undersides gray with pronounced row of black spots across wings.
Habitat　Woods, meadows, canyons.
Flight period　One, March–July.
Distribution　East to west in Canada, and in north of United States.

Xerces Blue

Glaucopsyche lygdamus xerces

♂♀♂

Identification Male with silver-blue uppers, dark border, female dark brown uppers, undersides with wavy row of white spots crossing wings, subspecies of *G. lygdamus*, also thought to have had true species status.
Habitat Coastal dunes. **Flight period** One, March–April.
Distribution Became extinct in 1943.

Northern Blue

Lycaeides idas

♂♀♂

Identification Male bright blue, highlighted veins, dots around margin of hindwing, female brown uppers with row of orange lunules round margin of hindwing and orange brushing across forewing, underside with orange lunules around wings.
Habitat Mountains, heaths, bogs, clearings.
Flight period One, June–August.
Distribution Alaska to Maine and south to Wisconsin.

Orange-bordered Blue *Lycaeides melissa*

♂♀

Identification Male blue uppers, female two-thirds forewing brown with blue at base, hindwing mostly blue with pronounced orange lunules, underside pale with orange band.
Habitat Lupine- and alfalfa-dominated habitats.
Flight period Two, May–August.
Distribution Western United States northeast to Maine, north well into Canada.

Greenish Blue

Plebejus saepiolus ♂♀♀

Identification Male silver-blue uppers with dark margins, sometimes greenish hue, female either brown or blue uppers, undersides fawn spotted all over with dark markings.
Habitat Roadsides, meadows, bogs.
Flight period One–two, June–July.
Distribution Alaska to Maine, northwestern United States.

Glandon Blue

Plebejus glandon ♂♀♂

Identification Male silvery-blue uppers, female brownish, underside white-blue with prominent spots on forewings, arrowhead marks on edge of underside of hindwing, variable as subspecies.
Habitat Woodland and prairie.
Flight period One, July–August.
Distribution One of few species with distribution along northern coast of Greenland, most of Canada, south to New Mexico and California.

Primrose Blue/
High Mountain

♂♀♀

Plebejus glandon franklinii

Identification Sexes similar, male slightly paler drab than female, undersides brown highlighted with light wedges and black spots.
Habitat Tundra and meadows.
Flight period One, June–August.
Distribution Wide range and well within Arctic Circle, from California to North Greenland and Newfoundland.

♂♀♀

Saltbush/San Emigdio *Plebulina emigdionis*

Identification   Male bluish-purple with broad dark borders on uppers, female strong orange suffusion around margin of wings and brown background, underside light with black spots in male, yellowish in female.
Habitat   Washes.
Flight period   Continuous, April–September.
Distribution   Southern California endemic.

Lupine/Common Blue *Icaricia icariodes*

♂♀

Identification   Male silver-blue within dark margins of uppers, female with blue scales at base of brown uppers, light underside with black spots, subspecies.
Habitat   Lupine-dominated areas.
Flight period   One, April–August.
Distribution   Western United States northward into Canada.

♂♀♀

Cushion-plant Blue/Shasta *Icaricia shasta*

Identification   Male violet within pronounced dark border of forewing, female violet within unpronounced dark margin of forewing, orange lunules around hindwing of both sexes, underside light brown with black spots.
Habitat   Mountains, meadows, clearings.
Flight period   One, July.
Distribution   Northwestern United States to Saskatchewan.

Silver-studded Blue/Acmon *Icaricia acmon*

Identification   Male violet uppers, female larger and with brown uppers, both sexes with orange lunules around margin of hindwing, undersides gray with orange lunules on hindwing, subspecies.
Habitat   Very catholic in its choice.
Flight period   Continuous, February–October.
Distribution   Western states from Mexico to British Columbia.

Large Silver-studded Blue/Lupine Blue
Icaricia lupini

Identification   Male violet uppers within dark margins, hindwing margins with orange lunules, female brown uppers and broad band of orange lunules around margin of hindwing, undersides fawn speckled with dark spots and orange lunules.
Habitat   Chaparral, canyons.   **Flight period**   One, May–July.
Distribution   California, Nevada, Oregon, Washington.

Cranberry Blue/ Yukon
Vacciniina optilete

Identification   Male violet uppers with dark margins, female darker throughout, underside light, spotted, and three orange marks at base of hindwing.
Habitat   Tundra and bogs.   **Flight period**   One, July.
Distribution   Canadian northwest and Alaska.

SKIPPERS

*T*hese are the smallest and most numerous of the butterflies which have exploited North America's great grassy plains. They have swept-back wings and are highly agile fliers. Their short antennae end in a hooked club, which marks them out from any other group of butterflies; in fact, some people do not even class them as butterflies because of their primitive nature. The giant skippers are an interesting group with many sub-tropical connections.

♂♀

Yucca/Yucca Giant Skipper *Megathymus yuccae*

Identification   White wedge toward tip of forewings is key
feature, male smaller than female with fewer orange markings
on upper hindwings, variable as subspecies.
Habitat   Yucca-rich deserts and scrubby woodland.
Flight period   One, January–June.
Distribution   East to west across southern states.

♀

♂

Desert Yucca/ Ursine Giant Skipper
Megathymus ursus

Identification   The largest skipper species, female with large
orange mark on forewing, and unmarked brown hindwings,
variable as species.
Habitat   Deserts, grassy and scrubby areas.
Flight period   One, April–August.
Distribution   Arizona, Texas.

♂♀

♂

Plains Yucca/
Strecker's Giant Skipper

Megathymus streckeri

Identification   Female larger than male, whitish-cream markings on forewing, and pale straw markings as row and on margin of hindwing, row absent in male, distinctive long hairs on upper hindwing and lower forewing, variable as subspecies.
Habitat   Prairie and open woodland.
Flight period   One, May–July.
Distribution   Montana to Texas and eastward to Nevada.

Manfreda Giant Skipper

Stallingsia smithi

Identification   Uppers dark brown in both sexes, female with thin row of orange marks around inside margin of uppers, absent from male hindwing, female larger with rounder forewing.
Habitat   Thorn forest.
Flight period   Two, April–October.
Distribution   Texas.

♂♀

$\male\female\female$

Southern Yucca/Cofaqui Giant Skipper

Megathymus cofaqui

Identification   Broad orange marks cross center of forewing, more extensive and brighter orange in female, and orange bar on hindwing, very long hairs on upper hindwing and lower forewing, variable as subspecies.
Habitat   Desert, woods and scrub.
Flight period   One–two, April–November.
Distribution   Florida, Georgia.

$\male\female\male$

Tawny/Orange Giant Skipper

Agathymus neumoegeni

Identification   Very orange on uppers, with more orange on uppers of larger female, with dark bar around margin of all wings, variable as subspecies.
Habitat   Desert with agave foodplant.
Flight period   One, September–October.
Distribution   Arizona, New Mexico, Texas.

♂♀

Arizona/Aryxna Giant Skipper

Agathymus aryxna

Identification Female uppers with slightly more orange marks than male, variable as subspecies.
Habitat Open grassy desert with scrub and agave foodplant.
Flight period August–November.
Distribution Arizona, New Mexico, Mexico.

♂♀♂

Canyonlands Giant Skipper *Agathymus alliae*

Identification Upper forewings of female heavily suffused in orange, with dark, angular, smudges, orange marks of male tend to be separate, underside less heavily marked, variable as subspecies.
Habitat Desert and wooded canyons.
Flight period One, August–October.
Distribution California, Nevada, Arizona, New Mexico.

$\male\female$

Huachuca Giant
$\male$ Skipper/Brigadier
Agathymus evansi

Identification   One of the largest and darkest of giant skippers, named after only habitat in which it is found, the Huachuca mountains.
Habitat   Canyons and mountains.
Flight period   One, August–October.
Distribution   Arizona, New Mexico.

$\male\female\female$

Little Giant Skipper   *Agathymus polingi*

Identification   Small size is key to identification, as well as its association with Arizona and Huachuca skippers.
Habitat   Open desert with woodland.
Flight period   One, September–October.
Distribution   Arizona, New Mexico and southward.

Lechuguilla/ Pecos Giant Skipper

Agathymus mariae

Identification Large yellow-orange markings in female as incomplete row, smaller in male, against light brown background color, variable as subspecies.

Habitat Rocky hills and slopes.

Flight period One, September–November.

Distribution New Mexico and Texas southward.

♂♀

♂♀♂

California Giant Skipper

Agathymus stephensi

Identification Large butterfly, underside with pale cream spots in loose row, and margin of brown uppers with pronounced checkering. Only giant skipper found in southern California, variable as subspecies.

Habitat Desert and scrub.

Flight period One, September–October.

Distribution Southern California southward into Baja California.

Arctic Skipperling/Skipper

Carterocephalus palaemon

Identification Crisp features, rich orange and warm brown on uppers, bright yellow-gray on underside hindwing.
Habitat Grassy areas and waysides.
Flight period One, May–July.
Distribution East to west coast across north of North America.

Swarthy Skipper

Nastra lherminier

Identification Dark all over forewings and unspotted, except for male sex brand, darker in female, underside fuscous to chestnut.
Habitat Grassy areas.
Flight period Two, June–September.
Distribution Maine to Florida and east to Mississippi.

Dingy Spotted/ Three-spotted Skipper

Cymaenes tripunctus

Identification Male with pointed forewings, otherwise sexes similar, 3–4 spots on forewing, two large, one or two small ones on otherwise dingy or fuscous wings, underside same color as topside.
Habitat Grassy areas.
Flight period February–November.
Distribution Tip of Florida only.

Least Skipperling

 ♂♀♀

Ancycloxypha numitor

Identification Uppers dark with orange patch on hindwing and flush on forewing but not prominent in male, large expanse of pale orange-tan on hindwings, forewings darker toward base.
Habitat Grassy meadows.
Flight period Several, February–December.
Distribution Most of eastern United States to west of Mississippi, and southern/eastern Canada.

Western/ Garita Skipperling

 ♂♀♀

Oarisma garita

Identification Fuscous over all wings, with reddish leading edge of forewing, underside hindwing gray with pale orange, underside forewing orange at tip, commonest skipper of the Rockies.
Habitat Meadows and grassland.
Flight period One, June–August.
Distribution Southern Canada, west of Great Lakes and south to Mexico.

Tiny Skipper/ Southern Skipperling

 ♂♀♂

Copaeodes minima

Identification One of the smallest of tan-colored skippers, with key muffled-white stripe through underside of hindwings.
Habitat Grassy areas and waysides.
Flight period Two, May–September.
Distribution Southeastern states of United States from Georgia to Texas into Mexico.

Western Tiny/
Orange Skipper

♂♀♀

Copaeodes aurantica

Identification   Light brown-tan wings on both surfaces, without white stripe on underside of hindwing.
Habitat   Grassy areas.
Flight period   Several, April–December.
Distribution   Southwestern states of United States east to Texas, and southward.

European
Skipperling

♂♀♂

Thymelicus lineola

Identification   Tawny-brown background color, with black veins toward margin of wings and dark border, undersides tawny-green, underside of antennal tip black.
Habitat   Grassy places and waysides.
Flight period   One, June–August.
Distribution   East coast of United States and Canada spreading westward.

White-veined/
Uncas Skipper

Hesperia uncas   ♂♀

Identification   Tawny-brown background color with yellow flecks toward margin of forewing, repeated on underside, underside hindwing distinctive with several silver marks, female larger.
Habitat   Grassy and sagebrush areas.
Flight period   Two or three, May–September.
Distribution   Central and western United States and southern Canada.

Jagged-border/Juba Skipper *Hesperia juba*

Identification   Bright forewings with marked orange area with dark center, sex brand in male, underside a greenish hue with cream spots, female slightly larger, variable as subspecies.
Habitat   Desert, sagebrush, chaparral.
Flight period   Two, May–September.
Distribution   British Columbia to California, and east to Colorado.

Holarctic Grass Skipper/Common Branded Skipper

Hesperia comma

Identification   Rich brown uppers in both sexes, undersides mottled green and yellow, male with distinctive sex brand, very variable as subspecies.
Habitat   Grassy areas, clearings, and waysides.
Flight period   One, June–August.
Distribution   Alaska to Baja California and across to Newfoundland.

Prairie/Ottoe Skipper *Hesperia ottoe*

Identification   Brown uppers and light brown margins, male sex brand prominent, female darker, even lighter underside markings.
Habitat   Grassy areas and prairie.
Flight period   One, June–July.
Distribution   Central United States and into southern Canada.

♂♀♂

Blazing Star Skipper/Leonardus Skipper

Hesperia leonardus

Identification   Dark butterfly, darker in female, male with orange markings on uppers, female pale orange spots, and male with subdued sex brand, underside hindwing chestnut with light row of spots, variable as subspecies.
Habitat   Prairie and clearings.
Flight period   One, August–October.
Distribution   Central United States and southern Canada to east coast.

♂♀♀

Cobweb Skipper   *Hesperia metea*

Identification   White-gray cobwebbing of marks and gray veins on undersides is key feature which gives butterfly its name, otherwise uppers are dark brown with orange marks in male, white forewing marks in female, variable as subspecies.
Habitat   Clearings and grassy waysides.
Flight period   One, March–April.
Distribution   South and eastern United States, except coastal area and Florida.

Montane/ Nevada Skipper

Hesperia nevada ♂♀

Identification Forewings with orange at base, male with pronounced sex brand, brownish forewing tips with pale yellow marks on underside of hindwing.
Habitat Clearings, grassy waysides, and high meadows.
Flight period One, May–July.
Distribution British Columbia southward via scattered populations to Arizona.

Saltgrass/ Sandhill Skipper

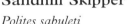

♂♀♂

Polites sabuleti

Identification Male very small, rich brown with black marks, especially male sex brand, and dark margins, orange suffused throughout but subdued in female, undersides have a washed-out look and lightly colored with silvery veining, variable as subspecies.
Habitat Grassy areas, even in urban sites.
Flight period One, June–August.
Distribution West coast from British Columbia to Baja California.

Yellow-patch Skipper

♂♀♂

Polites peckius

Identification Colorful butterfly with distinctive yellow-orange patches on upper hindwing of male, female slightly larger and darker with fewer orange marks on hindwing, underside or hindwing with pale yellow bands.
Habitat Prairie and meadows.
Flight period One, May–September.
Distribution Almost coast to coast, except west coastal area of British Columbia and Oregon.

Long Dash *Polites mystic*

Identification Uppers brown
with orange markings, underside
hindwing with long row of pale
streaks, male sex brand particularly
drawn-out, female forewing with
light yellow-orange marks.
Habitat Meadows and waysides.
Flight period One, May–September.
Distribution Almost coast to coast in southern Canada and
United States, except for coastal British Columbia and
Washington.

Tawny-edged Skipper

Polites themistocles

Identification Leading edge of
forewing toward base golden in
both sexes, contrasting with dark
somber coloration elsewhere,
upper hindwing brown and
completely unmarked, male sex
brand prominent, undersides very light in comparison.
Habitat Grassy areas, even in urban sites.
Flight period One, June–August.
Distribution Coast to coast in southern Canada and
northern United States, tailing off toward the western coast.

Brown Broken/ Northern Broken Dash

Wallengrenia egeremet

Identification A dark fuscous butterfly with feint light dashes
cut in two on forewing, thus its name, underside a repeat of
upper pattern, underside of hindwing brown with suspicion of
pale line of yellow spots.
Habitat Wet woodlands and clearings.
Flight period One, May–September.
Distribution Southeastern United States, west to Mississippi
River.

Black-vein/ Delaware Skipper

Atrytone logan

♂♀

Identification   Female slightly larger than male with much heavier and darker markings, particularly with broad black margins and distinct veins on uppers, undersides pale, variable as subspecies.

Habitat   Grassy areas and woodland margins.

Flight period   One, February–October.

Distribution   Most of United States east of Mississippi, and southern Canada.

Northern Dimorphic/ Hobomok Skipper

Poanes hobomok

♂♀

Identification   Uppers of both sexes brown with pale yellow patch on forewing, male sex brand evident, and small mark in much the same place in female, females have two color forms (dimorphic), light and dark, underside hindwing of both sexes has yellowish patch, variable as subspecies.

Habitat   Grassy areas, including meadows and clearings.

Flight period   One, May–September.

Distribution   Saskatchewan to Nova Scotia, south to Georgia.

Dun Sedge/Sedge Witch Skipper

Euphyes vestris

Identification   Uniform dun color above and below, with few markings, except male sex brand and small white markings on upper forewing of female.
Habitat   Grassy waysides and clearings.
Flight period   Two, May–December.
Distribution   Throughout much of United States and southern Canada, but patchy distribution in western United States.

Black Little/Roadside Skipper

Amblyscirtes vialis

Identification   Very descriptive names for this small butterfly, which has tiny white marks near leading edge of forewings, checkered margins.
Habitat   Apart from roadsides, clearings and other grassy areas.
Flight period   One, May–September.
Distribution   West to east across northern United States, absent from southwest.

Silver-spotted Skipper *Epargyreus clarus*

Identification   As name suggests, a large silver spot is very obvious on underside of hindwing, wings are rich brown color, with orange forewing marks in male, and pale yellow in female.
Habitat   Clearings, prairies, and canyons.
Flight period   One, May–September.
Distribution   West to east United States with patchy distribution in southwest.

Cloudywing/Northern Cloudywing

Thorybes pylades

Identification   Brown-black above and below with small white marks dotted over forewing, variable as subspecies.
Habitat   Meadows and clearings.
Flight period   Two, March–December.
Distribution   From North West Territories to Florida and California.

Powdered/Texas Powdered Skipper

Systasea pulverulenta

Identification   Highly distinctive hindwing shape, wings powdered with black scales over rich nut-brown color of uppers, undersides much lighter, pale yellow to gray.
Habitat   Mountain waysides and ridges.
Flight period   Several, February–December.
Distribution   Texas southward.

Aspen/Dreamy Duskywing *Erynnis icelus*

Identification   Warm mottled-gray uppers with wavy rows of light marks on outer part of forewing, underside uniform light brown, with bands of tiny pale marks.
Habitat   Clearings and wet meadows.
Flight period   One, May–June.
Distribution   From north of North West Territories to Georgia and Arizona.

Banded Oak/ Sleepy Duskywing

Erynnis brizo

♂♀♂

Identification Mottled gray forewings, with distinct wavy band, hindwing light brown with rows of faint spots toward margin, variable as subspecies.
Habitat Woodland. **Flight period** One, March–April.
Distribution Eastern United States northward, irregular distribution in southwest.

Eastern Oak/ Juvenal's Duskywing

Erynnis juvenalis

♂♀

Identification Forewing gray-brown and dingy with series of zig-zag marks, speckled with groups of tiny white marks near tip, hindwing mottled brown, with distinct fringe throughout.
Habitat Oak woodlands.
Flight period Two, April–September.
Distribution East of Mississippi River and into southern Canada.

Hairy/Persius Duskywing

Erynnis persius

♂♀

Identification Dingy colors on uppers, with tiny light marks on forewing tip, undersides lighter brown.
Habitat Grasslands and open woodland.
Flight period Two, May–September.
Distribution Mostly western Canada and western United States, with populations also in eastern United States.

Northern Grizzled/Alpine Checkered Skipper

Pyrgus centaurea

Identification   Distinct checkered margin of all wings, uppers black with white spots, underside brown-olive with light suffusions, variable as subspecies.
Habitat   Flowery meadows, clearings.
Flight period   One, April–August.
Distribution   Northern Alaska to Newfoundland, Carolinas.

Checkered/ Common Checkered Skipper

Pyrgus communis

Identification   Male more heavily checkered over uppers than female, underside very pale with similar checkered pattern and distinct off-white band, variable as subspecies.
Habitat   Many and various.
Flight period   Numerous, all year in Texas.
Distribution   Most of United States, northward into southern Canada.

Common Sooty Wing/ Roadside Rambler

Pholisora catullus

Identification   Small black butterfly with rounded wings and black underside, with a few tiny white variable spots on forewing.
Habitat   Disturbed ground and urban areas.
Flight period   Two, May–September.
Distribution   Most of United States, especially California and Baja California.

Index